SIMPLY Sewing

SECOND BOOK

LEILA AITKEN

Collins Glasgow and London

ABOUT THIS BOOK

This book includes all you need to know to make your own clothes. All the main dressmaking processes are here – from cutting out to turning up the hem.

Six easy graph patterns are given in the book to form a basic wardrobe – a nightdress and a housecoat, a wrap skirt, a sweater dress or top, a special occasion dress and a luxury travel coat. These involve only the simplest dressmaking procedures.

Then you can progress to the use of paper patterns; seven are discussed in detail and these sections include a series of sewing lessons describing the more advanced dressmaking techniques.

It should be possible to start on the first simple pattern given in the book – the housecoat – and by following the teaching given with each garment, to progress to the fully lined couture suit in the last chapter.

Step by step directions are illustrated with numerous line drawings and diagrams of basic sewing/dressmaking techniques such as putting in a zip and turning up a hem evenly and invisibly.

AUTHOR'S NOTE

I should like to thank Bob Christie of Grampian Television and David Skinner of STYLE Patterns without whose help I could not have written this book.
It is dedicated, with love, to Alice, to my family and to my husband without whose tolerance and affection this book would not even have been started.

COLOUR ILLUSTRATIONS

First published 1981 by William Collins Sons & Co Ltd in association with Grampian Television and STYLE Patterns.
© Leila Aitken 1981.
© Photographs and drawings STYLE Patterns 1981.
Designed by Youé and Spooner Limited.
Filmset by Jolly & Barber Ltd, Rugby.
Printed in Great Britain by William Collins Sons & Co. Ltd.

ISBN 0 00 411630 5

MAKING THE PATTERN

Using dressmaker's squared paper ready ruled into 5cm squares, copy the pattern given in the diagram so that the outline in each square corresponds exactly. Mark the notches. Cut out the pattern. This is the short version of the housecoat.

To lengthen the pattern to make the full length version, pin a sheet of paper (approximately 50cm wide and 45cm long) to the hem of the front and back pattern pieces. Using a long ruler, continue the lines of the pattern at each side for 40cm. Draw the hem line in a curve parallel to the original line. *Diagram 1.* Lengthen the facing piece at the hem by 40cm in the same way.

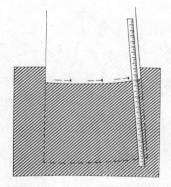

1 lengthening the front or back of the short version

CUTTING OUT

Follow the cutting layout given for the appropriate fabric width. Fabric 115cm wide is not quite wide enough for the width of the sleeve in sizes 14–16. For these sizes, open out the fabric and cut the sleeves singly, one slightly above the other. Reverse the pattern for one of the sleeves or you will have two identical sleeves for the same arm! Cut two strips for the belt 13cm wide across the width of the fabric as shown in the cutting layout. 1.5cm turnings are allowed throughout.

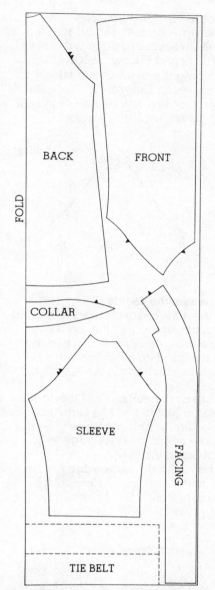

cutting layout *150–160cm wide fabric (without nap) short version*

cutting layout *for sleeves sizes 14–16 115cm wide fabric*

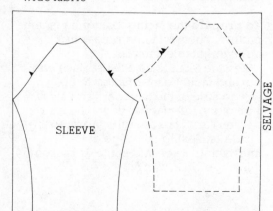

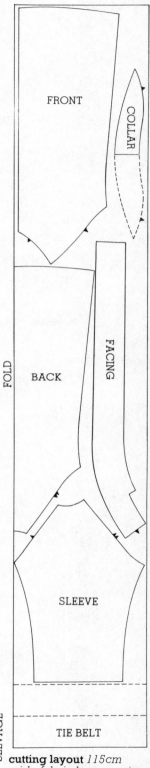

cutting layout *115cm wide fabric long version*

SEWING INSTRUCTIONS

With right sides together, join the armhole seam of the sleeve pieces to the front and the back pieces, matching the notches and taking a 1.5cm seam. *Diagram 2*. Press the seam turnings towards the centre front and centre back.

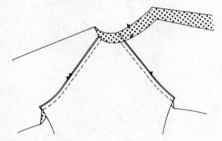

2 putting in the sleeves

To neaten the seams Trim the underneath seam allowance to 3mm. Turn under 3mm of the top seam allowance, and tack down to conceal the trimmed turning. Hand hem or machine stitch in place. *Diagram 3*.

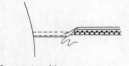

3 neatening seams

To attach the collar Fold the collar piece in half to find the centre back of the collar. With right sides together pin the notched collar edge to the garment at the centre back. Pin the collar along the neck edge easing to fit and matching the notches on the garment fronts. Stitch the seam and press the turnings upwards. *Diagram 4*.

4 attaching the collar

To prepare the facing Using the facing pattern, cut two facing pieces in lightweight interfacing.

Lay the facings on a flat surface and pin and tack the interfacing to the wrong side of the facings. Trim away 1cm of the interfacing down the inside curve. Turn 1cm over the fabric to the inside enclosing the edge of the interfacing. Tack and stitch 6mm from this edge. *Diagram 5*.

5 turning in facing

With right sides together, join the short back neck seam of the facing. *Diagram 6*. Cut away the interfacing in the seam allowance close to the stitching line and press the seam open.

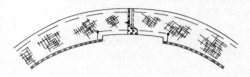

6 joining back neck seam

With right sides together, pin the facing to the garment, matching the centre back of the collar to the facing seam. Tack and stitch right round the collar and down the fronts, taking a 1.5cm seam. *Diagram 7*.

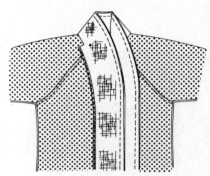

7 stitching facing to collar and fronts

Trim away the interfacing in the seam allowance. Trim the seam to 6mm. Turn the facing to the inside. Work the seam between the finger and thumb so that the seam line lies exactly on the edge. Tack in place close to the edge and press well.

To finish the inside neck edge of the collar Clip the corners at each side of the centre back seam of the collar facing to a depth of 1.5cm. *Diagram 8*.

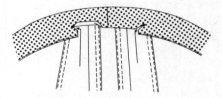

8 clipping collar corners

Turn under 1.5cm between the clips and bring this edge down to the line of machine stitching and hand hem in place. Turn under the remaining raw edge of the facing and hem it on to the sleeve seam. *Diagram 9.*

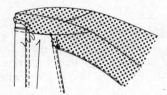

9 turning in facing edge

Fold the garment in half so that the back and front are together with right sides facing, and stitch the side and the underarm seam. *Diagram 10.*

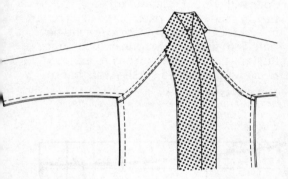

10 stitching side and underarm seam

Turn up the hem to the desired length. Finish, following the instructions given on pages 43 to 46.

Top stitch the fronts and the roll collar. Follow the instructions on page 46.

Press and remove tacking threads.

To form the cuffs Press under 1cm on the raw edge of the sleeve. Turn under a further turning of 9cm. Stitch in place. *Diagram 11.* Turn back a 7cm deep cuff to the right side of the sleeve. Press. Top stitch the edge of the cuff. *Diagram 12.* Stitch the cuff to the sleeve at the underarm seam to hold it in place.

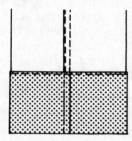

11 stitching sleeve turning

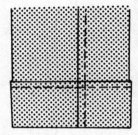

12 top stitching cuff

The belt
Join the belt pieces together across one short side. Fold the belt in half with the right side to the inside. Stitch across both ends and 1.5cm away from the raw edge, leaving a break of about 5cm in the stitching line. *Diagram 13.*

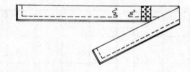

13 stitching belt

Trim the seams to 6mm. Turn inside out through the opening. Slip stitch the opening together. Press. Top stitch the belt.

Wrap Skirt

This is a very easy pattern to make. There are no fitting problems and the waistband fastens with Velcro fastening and a narrow tie belt. (Photograph page 21.)

A wrap skirt is the easiest type of skirt to make and it is an unrestricting casual style to wear. The skirt gathers into soft folds at the centre front and back, but the gathers are kept well away from the hips at the sides, to give a slim outline.

MATERIAL REQUIRED
1.60 metres fabric 140–150cm wide
1 metre fold-a-band waist interfacing 4cm wide
2 strips of soft iron-on interfacing 70cm × 4cm for the edge of the overlap
   The finished length of this skirt is 70cm with a 4cm hem.

MAKING THE PATTERN
Using dressmaker's squared paper, ready marked into 5cm squares, copy the pattern given in the diagram so that the outline in each square corresponds exactly. Mark the position of the notches and the cutting line for the left front. Cut out the pattern.

CUTTING OUT
Follow the cutting layout given, placing the centre back of the skirt to the fold. Cut a strip of fabric for the tie belt, 7cm wide, down one selvage, the full length of the fabric. Leave the remaining fabric to cut the waistband

pattern layout
sizes 10 and 12 ——————— *solid line*
sizes 14 and 16 – – – – – – *broken line*
1 square = 5 cm

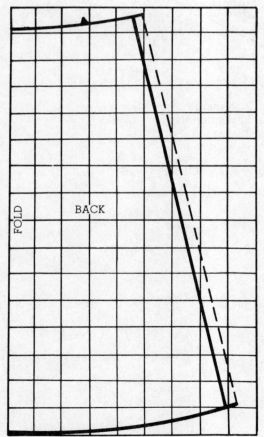

FOLD BACK

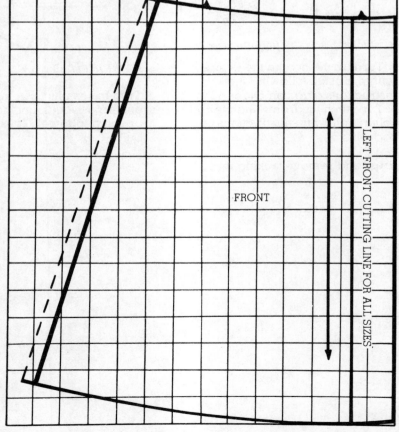

FRONT

LEFT FRONT CUTTING LINE FOR ALL SIZES

once the length required has been checked against the skirt. On the left front only, cut off the surplus fabric down the straight edge on the line marked on the pattern.

Mark the position of the notches on the fabric when cutting out. 1.5cm turnings are allowed throughout.

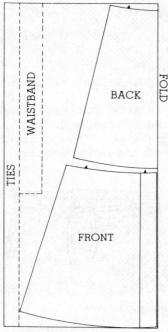

cutting layout
140–150cm wide fabric

SEWING INSTRUCTIONS
On both skirt fronts, place the strip of soft iron-on interfacing on the wrong side 6mm away from the straight edge of the skirt fronts. Press, using a damp cloth and a hot, dry iron.

Use an up and down pressing movement with the iron, not an ironing movement, and press heavily to give a good bond between fabric and interfacing. Turn 6mm to the wrong side to overlap the edge of the interfacing and edge stitch to neaten the seam. *Diagram 1.*

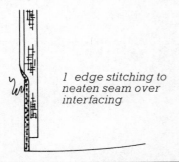

1 edge stitching to neaten seam over interfacing

Fold back this interfaced strip to the inside so that the interfacing is concealed. Tack. *Diagram 2.*

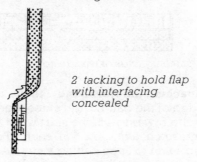

2 tacking to hold flap with interfacing concealed

On the back skirt and the *right* front skirt only 6mm away from the raw edge, make a row of very small running stitches between the notches. Pull up the fabric into even gathers with the thread so that the distance between the notches measures 18cm. Cut two strips of 6mm tape 18cm long. Tack the tape over the gathers and machine stitch along the centre of the tape to hold the gathers securely in place. *Diagram 3.*

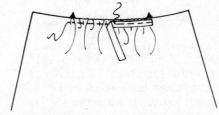

3 tacking tape in place over gathers

With right sides together, tack and stitch the side seams taking a 1.5cm seam. Press open.

The waistband
Measure the waist edge of the skirt. Cut a strip of fabric for the waistband this length plus 3cm for turnings and 11cm wide.

Cut the fold-a-band to the length of the waistband strip less 3cm.

Fold the waistband in half along its length. Press. Place the notched fold line of the interfacing over the fold on the wrong side of the waistband. Press heavily using a damp cloth and hot, dry iron.

Turn up 1.5cm turning over the interfacing down one long side only.

Fold the band with right sides to the inside and stitch across, taking a 1.5cm

The length of the waistband will vary from approximately 90cm in the smaller sizes to 100cm in the larger sizes.

seam. *Diagram 4*. Trim the seam to 6mm. Cut off the corner and turn the ends right side out. Press.

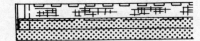

4 stitching ends of waistband

Attaching the waistband Pin the raw edge of the band, right sides together, to the raw edge of the skirt waist. Tack and stitch taking a 1.5cm seam. Trim the seam to 6mm cutting away the tape holding the gathers in place. Bring the folded edge down on to the stitching line concealing the turnings and hem in place. *Diagram 5*.

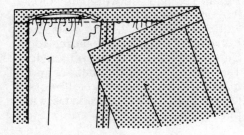

5 hemming the waistband

Try on the skirt and mark the position of each end of the overlap with a pin. Attach a 2.5cm strip of Velcro fastening at each end of the overlap to hold it securely.

The tie belt
Cut the strip of fabric in two. Fold the strips in half lengthwise. Stitch down the long side and across one end only taking a 1.5cm seam. *Diagram 6*. Trim the seams to 6mm. Use a blunt bodkin to turn the ties right side out. Press with the seam line on the edge. Top stitch the ties very close to the edge. *Diagram 7*.

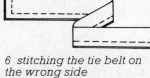

6 stitching the tie belt on the wrong side

7 top stitching the tie belt

Attaching the ties Turn in 6mm at the raw edge of tie. Pin the tie to the waistband at the side seams, open end pointing towards the centre front. *Diagram 8*.

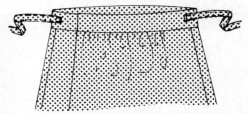

8 stitching the ties to the waistband

Stitch with two rows of stitching. Fold the tie on itself with the long end towards the centre front and stitch again with one row of stitching. *Diagram 9*.

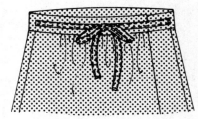

9 top stitching the ties

Finish the hem following the instructions on pages 43 to 46. Open out the overlap to stitch the hem and then slip stitch in place. *Diagram 10*.

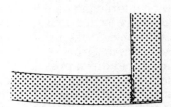

10 slip stitching the overlap of the hem

Nightdress

This is a soft pretty nightdress, but unlike so many glamorous nighties this one will keep you warm. It is simplicity itself to make up as it has only three pattern pieces; a cross-over bodice cut in one with a short cape sleeve, a back and front pieces which overlap off centre to form a slit seam which is trimmed with lace.

MATERIAL REQUIRED
2.70 metres fabric 115cm wide
5.50m lace approximately 3cm wide

MAKING THE PATTERN
Using dressmaker's squared paper, ready ruled into 5cm squares, copy the pattern given in the diagram so that the outline in each square corresponds exactly. Mark the notches. Cut out the pattern.

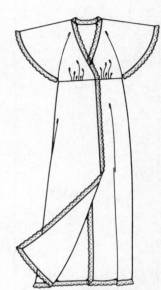

Use a slinky fabric with good draping qualities or a sheer polyester jersey to make up this nightie. (Photograph page 29.)

pattern layout
sizes 10 and 12 –––––––– broken line
sizes 14 and 16 ————— solid line
1 square = 5 cm

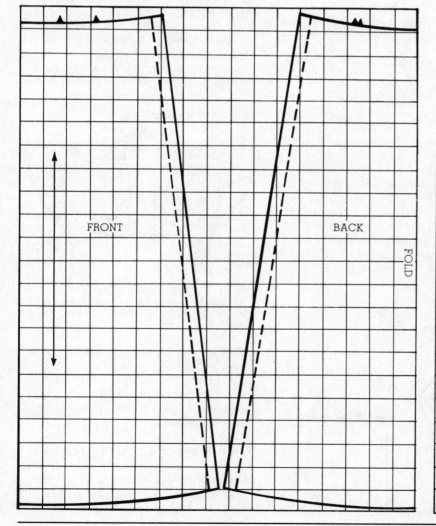

FRONT

BACK

FOLD

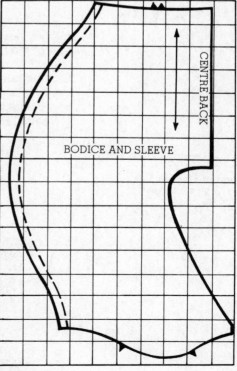

BODICE AND SLEEVE

CENTRE BACK

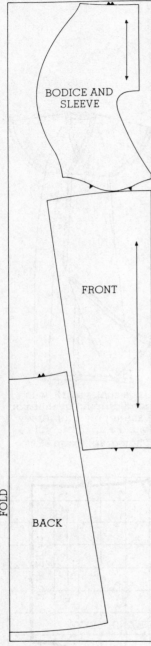

cutting layout
115cm wide fabric

CUTTING OUT
Following the cutting layout given, place the nightdress back to the fold and the other pieces with the arrow parallel to the selvages of the fabric. 1.5cm turnings are allowed throughout.

SEWING INSTRUCTIONS
With right sides together, join the centre back seam of the bodice taking a 1.5cm seam. Neaten the seam with a zig-zag stitch or an overcasting stitch close to the stitching line. Trim the surplus seam turnings away close to the stitching. *Diagram 1.*

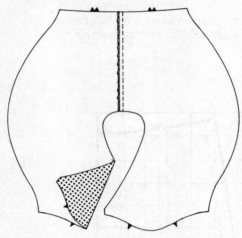

1 joining centre back seam of the bodice

Work a row of very small running stitches between the notches on each side of the front bodice 1cm from the edge. Ease the fabric with the thread to fit the notches at the top of the skirt front. Tack and stitch the skirt to the bodice, taking a 1.5cm seam. *Diagram 2.* Neaten and trim the seams.

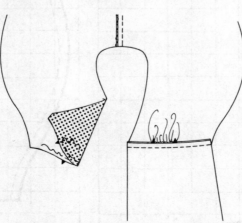

2 stitching skirt front to bodice over gathers

Run a gathering stitch between the notches on the skirt back. Draw up the fabric so that these notches fit the notches on the bodice back. Stitch the bodice to the skirt back taking a 1.5cm seam. *Diagram 3.* Neaten and trim the seam.

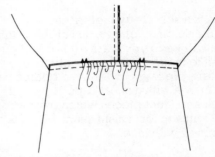

3 stitching skirt back to bodice over gathers

To attach the lace Press under 3mm on the neck edge of the bodice. Machine stitch very close to the edge. Turn under a further 6mm. Tack and press. Tack the edge of the lace just under the folded edge. Machine stitch very close to the edge.

Neaten and trim the edges of the sleeves in the same way. *Diagram 4.*

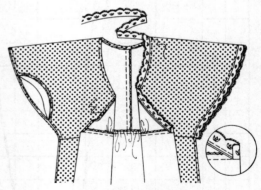

4 attaching lace to neckline and sleeves with (inset) enlarged detail showing centre front

On the right front edge of the skirt only, turn under 3mm to the wrong side. Press. Turn under a further 2.5cm. Tack and press. Stitch the lace down this front edge from the waist seam to the hem.

The side seams Lay the nightie on a flat surface and with right sides to the inside, pin the side seams together matching the bodice seams at both sides. Tack and stitch taking a 1.5cm seam and joining the edges of the lace also. *Diagram 5.* Neaten and trim the seams.

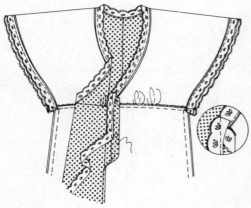

5 sewing side seams and tacking lace to front with (inset) enlarged detail showing join at waistline

Fitting the nightie Try on the nightie and wrap it round the body to overlap snugly at the front, but allowing sufficient ease for the nightie to slip on and off over the head comfortably. Pin in place.

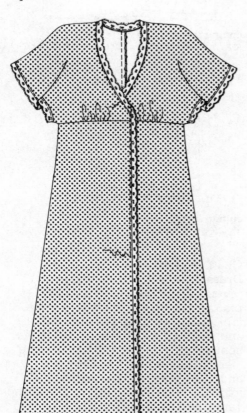

6 top stitching front seam over lace leaving opening

Stitch the front seam from the right side on top of the stitching attaching the lace leaving the seam open 60cm from the hem. *Diagram 6.* Trim away the surplus fabric on the inside of the seam to 2.5cm. Clip this seam at right angles to the stitching line where the stitching ends. *Diagram 7.*

To neaten the front slit Press under a 2.5cm turning on the left hand edge of the nightie front below the clip. Attach the lace trimming to the folded edge. Turn in a narrow turning on the remaining raw edge of the front seam and stitch close to the edge to neaten. Trim with lace. Strengthen at the clip by stitching across the top of the seam turnings and through to the fabric of the nightie. *Diagram 8.*

Finish the hem of the nightie with lace.

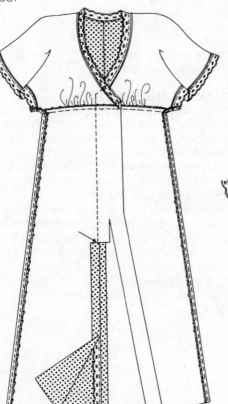

7 trimming surplus fabric from inside and clipping seam

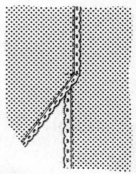

8 strengthening the fabric at the clip

To make the nightie fit more snugly under the bust without reducing the ease which allows it to slip on and off without a front opening, a length of soft elastic can be stitched to the back waist seam turning. Cut a length of narrow elastic the same length as the back waist seam less 5cm. Stretch the elastic the full length of the seam. Slip it behind the seam turning and stitch in place using a zig-zag stitch with the elastic extended so that it gathers in the fabric when relaxed. *Diagram 9.*

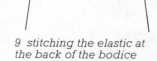

9 stitching the elastic at the back of the bodice

Simple Sweater Dress or Pull-on Top

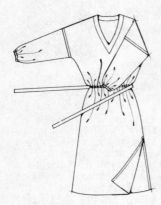

This very simple dress has been designed specifically for jersey fabrics, such as stretch velour, polyester or cotton jersey. It has a dropped waistline which is drawn in with elastic to give a bloused effect to the bodice. The skirt is straight with a side slit and the sleeve is three-quarter length. (Photograph page 17.)

MATERIAL REQUIRED
Dress 1.70 metres jersey fabric 150–160cm wide
bias binding
50cm stretch interfacing
Top 90cm jersey fabric 150–160cm wide
50cm stretch interfacing
1.60 metres cord

MAKING THE PATTERN
Using dressmaker's squared paper, ready marked into 5cm squares, copy the pattern given in the diagram so that the outline in each square corresponds exactly. Mark the casing line and the cutting line for the top. Cut out the pattern. Trace the shaded areas from the pattern following the neck curve to make separate patterns for the front and back neck facings. 1.5cm turnings are allowed throughout.

Cut the pattern across on the line marked to make the pattern for the top.

The pattern can be cut across on the line marked to make a pull-on blouson top and the sleeve omitted.

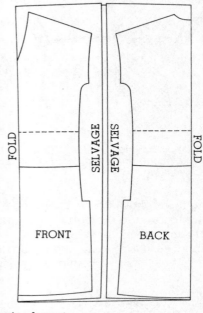

cutting layout
for 150–160cm wide fabric for sweater dress

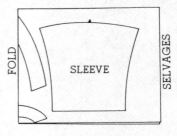

cutting layout
for sleeves and facings for sweater dress

CUTTING OUT
Dress Following the cutting layout given, cut out the sleeve and facings, placing the facings to the fold of the fabric. Open out the remaining fabric and re-fold it with the selvages to the centre, lying on the original fold line (see the cutting layout). Cut the back and front, placing them both to the fold. Mark the casing line on the fabric with tailor's tacks.

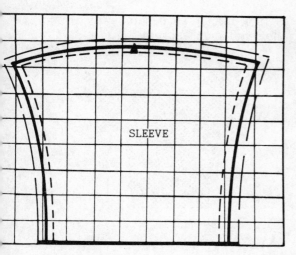

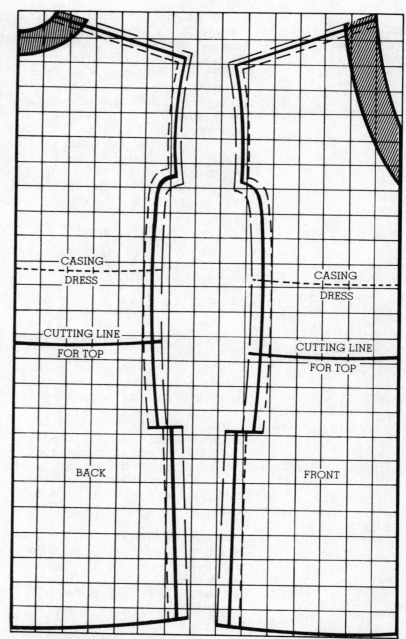

pattern layout
size 10 — — — — — — short broken lines
sizes 12 and 14 ————————— solid line
sizes 16 and 18 — — — — long broken lines
1 square = 5cm

Sleeveless top Open out the fabric
and re-fold it with the selvages to the
centre, lying on the original fold line
(see the cutting layout). Cut the facings
and back and front, placing all the
pieces to a fold as shown.

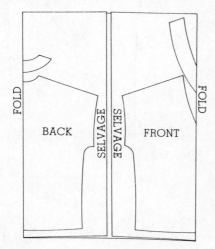

cutting layout
for pull-on top

SEWING INSTRUCTIONS
Dress Taking a 1.5cm seam, tack and
stitch the back and front together at the
shoulder. *Diagram 1*. Press the seam
open.

1 sewing back and front of dress

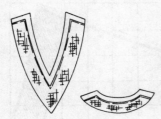

2 interfacing of the neck facings

4 stitching facing to neck edge

If the fabric is thick, e.g. a stretch velour, trim one of the turnings a little further to 3mm, so that the turnings are layered. This gives a flatter edge when pressed.

Top stitch through facing and garment 3cm away from the neck edge. *Diagram 5*. For top-stitching, see page 46.

5 top stitching garment and facing

Cut the back and front facing in iron-on stretch interfacing. Tack the interfacing to the wrong side of the facing pieces just inside the seam turning 1.5cm from the edge. Trim away the seam turnings on the interfacing at the shoulder seams and neck edge. *Diagram 2*. Bond the interfacing to the fabric using a damp cloth and hot iron. Join the facing pieces at the shoulder seams. Press the seams open. Neaten the outer edge of the facing using a zig-zag or overcasting stitch. *Diagram 3*.

3 neatening outer edges of joined facings

With right sides together, stitch the facing to the neck edge, taking a 1.5cm seam and matching the shoulder seams. *Diagram 4*.

Trim the seam to 6mm.

Clip the point of the V-shaped neckline almost to the stitching line. Turn the facing to the wrong side. Work the fabric between the finger and thumb so that the seam line lies exactly on the edge. Tack and press.

The sleeves With right sides together and taking a 1.5cm seam, stitch the sleeve to the armhole, matching the notch in the sleeve head to the shoulder seam. *Diagram 6*. Press the turnings towards the neckline.

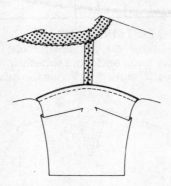

6 stitching sleeve to armhole

Tack and top-stitch 6mm away from the seam line. *Diagram 7*.

7 top stitching sleeve seam

The side seams With right sides together and taking a 1.5cm seam, stitch the side and underarm seams. Leave the left side seam open 40cm from the hem. Trim away the seam extension on the right side seam. *Diagram 8*. Press the seams open. Turn under a 3mm turning on the seam extension at the side slit. Press and edge stitch.

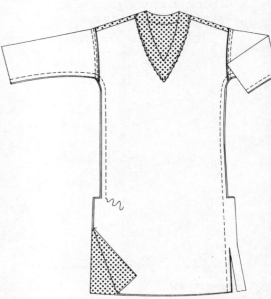

8 stitching side and underarm seams leaving 40cm from hem to left side and trimming seam extension on right side

Opposite: simple sweater dress and pull-on top

Measure and finish the hem following the instructions given on pages 43 to 46, opening out the seam extension to stitch the hem. Slip stitch the seam extension to the hem. *Diagram 10.* Top stitch the side slit, 6mm away from the fold and across the top. *Diagram 11.*

10 slip stitching seam extension to hem

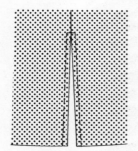

11 top stitching side slit

13 edge stitching sleeve casing leaving gap

Fold back the turning along the seam line. Tack and press. Invisibly slip stitch the turnings to the dress, finishing the stitching 8cm from the hem. *Diagram 9.*

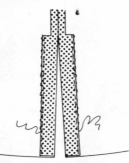

9 slip stitching turnings of side slit

The waist casing Catch stitch the side seam turnings to the garment at the casing line. This prevents the bodkin getting caught in the turnings when threading through the elastic. On the inside of the dress, pin and tack the bias binding on the casing line, turning under the ends at the join to neaten. Edge stitch at each side of the bias binding. *Diagram 12.* Using a bodkin, insert soft elastic through the casing. Adjust to fit, pin and cut off the surplus elastic. Oversew the ends of the elastic together. Slip stitch the opening in the casing.

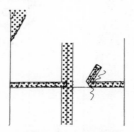

12 edge stitching bias binding for waist casing

The sleeve casing Press under 6mm on the lower edge of the sleeve. Turn under a further 1cm. Tack and edge stitch on each side of the hem, leaving a break in the stitching to insert the elastic. *Diagram 13.* Using a bodkin, thread soft elastic through the casing and adjust to fit. Oversew the ends of the elastic together and stitch the opening.

The belt
Wear a purchased belt or make a narrow tie belt from the strip of surplus fabric down the original fold line.

Cut the strip 8cm wide and follow the instructions given for the tie belt in the housecoat pattern on page 7.

SEWING INSTRUCTIONS
Pull on top. Follow the instructions above, omitting the waist casing, the belt and sleeves.

Slip stitch the seam turnings to the fabric at each side 4cm from the hem. Press under 6mm at the lower edge of the top. Turn up a further 1.5cm. Edge stitch each side of the hem. *Diagram 14.*

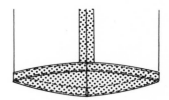

14 edge stitching side of top

On the right side of the garment, snip the thread to open up the seam within these lines of stitching.

Cut the cord into two equal lengths. Thread them through the casings at the back and front to draw up the garment at the hem and tie at the sides. Knot the ends of the cord. *Diagram 15.*

15 using cord to draw up the hem of the top

Finish the raw edge of the armhole with a narrow hem.

A Dress for an Occasion

This is a lovely dress. It drapes on to the figure in soft folds from a shoulder yoke into an elasticized waist and a flared, graceful skirt. The full batwing sleeves are cut in one with the bodice and are elasticized at the lower edge.

pattern layout
sizes 12 and 14 — — — — — — — broken line
sizes 16 and 18 —————— solid line
1 square = 5 cm

This is an easy pattern to make. It has only five pattern pieces and fitting problems are solved with concealed elastic! It is worn with a purchased belt.

(Photograph page 25.)

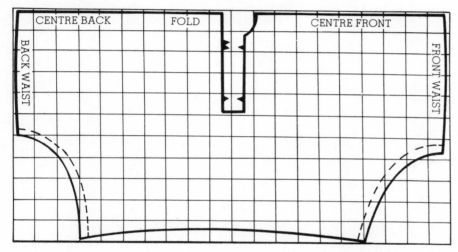

CHOOSING YOUR FABRIC

It is important to choose the right fabric for this pattern, one that falls into graceful folds. A fine polyester jersey is ideal, because this has just the right degree of stretch, it gathers into small bulk and does not crush. Soft fine cottons and fine wool blends are also suitable.

MATERIAL REQUIRED

3.70 metres fabric 115cm wide without nap or one way design
2.90 metres fabric 165cm wide without nap or one way design

MAKING THE PATTERN

Using dressmaker's squared paper, ready ruled into 5cm squares, copy the pattern given in the diagram so that the outline in each square corresponds exactly. Mark the notches. Cut out the pattern. 1.5cm turnings are allowed throughout.

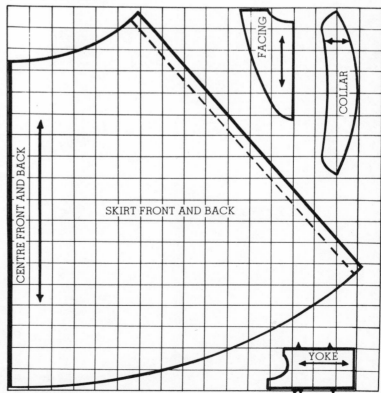

*Over: left, wrap style towelling robe and housecoat
right, wrap skirts*

CUTTING OUT

Keep the fabric in its lengthwise fold and cut out the bodice with the centre back to the fold. In the 165cm fabric, cut the front facing and shoulder yokes as well. The yoke piece is cut twice. Open out the remaining fabric, fold it across the width and cut the skirt piece twice with the arrow parallel to the selvages. Cut the collar and, in the 115cm fabric, cut the yoke piece (twice) and the front facing. Cut round the notches given. From the remaining fabric cut 2 strips 40cm long and 4cm wide for the neck ties.

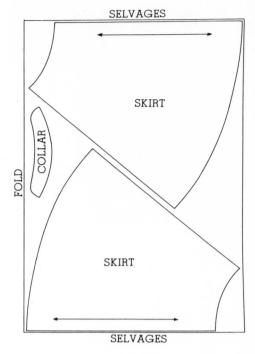

cutting layout *115cm wide fabric*

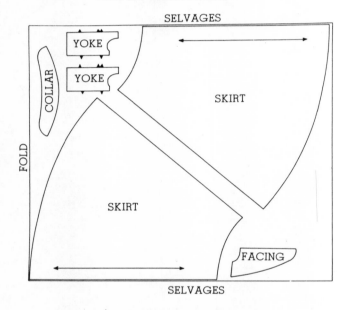

cutting layout *165cm wide fabric*

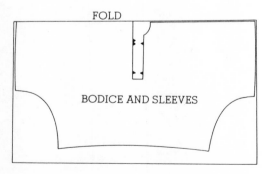

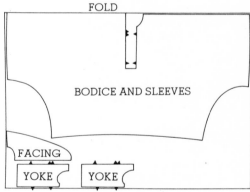

SEWING INSTRUCTIONS

The shoulder yoke Work a row of very small running stitches 1cm from the cut edge between the notches at the back and front shoulders on the bodice. *Diagram 1.*

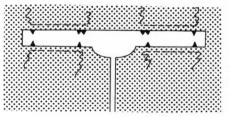

1 working the rows of gathering stitches between the notches on the bodice

Press and tack a 1.5cm turning to the wrong side on the straight edges of the yokes. *Diagram 2.*

Pull up the gathering thread on the back and front shoulders until the notches on the yoke fit the corresponding shoulder notches. (The double notch is on the back.) Lay the bodice flat on a table right side uppermost. Place two of the yoke pieces over the shoulders right side uppermost, matching the notches. Tack and stitch round the edges of the yoke. *Diagram 3.*

2 turning in the straight edges of the yokes

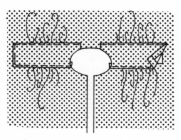

3 tacking and stitching yoke pieces on right side over gathers

The ties Cut a length of thin cord 50cm long. Fold the strip of fabric for the ties in half over the cord, with the right side to the inside. Stitch the cord securely to the fabric of the tie at one end and stitch down the length of the tie (taking care not to catch the cord in the stitching) taking a 1cm seam. *Diagram 4.*

4 stitching the ties

Turn the tie right side out by pulling the end of the cord to ease the fabric through to the right side. Cut off the cord. Make two ties in this way. Do not press them. Neaten the ends by turning in the raw edges and oversewing them.

Pin the ties to the centre front opening 2cm down from the neck curve. With right sides together pin and tack the front facings to the bodice fronts at the neck edge. Stitch to within 4cm of the bottom edge. *Diagram 5.*

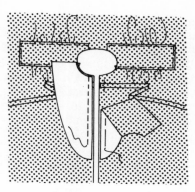

5 stitching facings and ties to bodice front

Trim the seams and turn the facings to the inside. Tack along the seam edge to hold it in place. Press.

Neaten the inside of the dress at the shoulder by placing the other two yoke pieces, right sides uppermost, to cover the raw edges of the first yokes. Slip hem in position. Join the centre front seam taking a 1.5cm turning. Avoid catching in the front facings. Slip stitch the bottom edge of the facings to the centre front seam.

The collar Cut a collar shape in lightweight interfacing – preferably stretch interfacing for a jersey fabric. Tack the interfacing to the wrong side of one collar piece. Press under 1.5cm on the neck edge of the remaining piece. *Diagram 6.* With right sides together, pin the collar pieces together and tack and stitch round the outer curve of the collar. *Diagram 7.*

6 pressing turning on neck edge of collar

7 stitching round outer edge of collar

Trim the seam to approximately 4mm. Turn the collar right side out. Tack round the outer edge to keep the seam line exactly on the edge. Press.

Fold the collar in half and mark half way with a pin. With right sides together place the collar to the neck edge, with the pin matching the centre back of the bodice. Pin the front collar edges to the centre fronts of the dress.

Pin round the rest of the neck curve easing to fit. Stitch, taking a 1.5cm seam. Trim the seam to 6mm and clip the curves. Bring the folded edge of the collar down to the stitching line and slip stitch in place. *Diagram 8.*

8 slip stitching inside of collar

Stitch the underarm seams of the bodice and clip the curves. *Diagram 9.*

9 stitching underarm seams and clipping curves

Press the seams open. Press under 6mm on the lower sleeve edges. Turn under a further 1.5cm forming a hem. Stitch close to both edges of the hem. Leave a break in the stitching to insert the elastic. Thread soft elastic through the hem, using a bodkin. *Diagram 10.* Draw up the sleeve hems to fit. Cut off the surplus elastic and stitch the ends together.

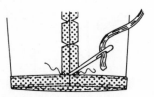

10 threading soft elastic through sleeve hem

The skirt
Stitch the four skirt pieces together taking a 1.5cm seam. Press the seams open. *Diagram 11.*

With right sides together, pin and tack the bodice waistline to the skirt waistline, easing to fit. Stitch, taking 1.5cm seam. Press the turnings upwards. Make a second row of stitching through the bodice and the turnings together forming a casing. Leave a break in the stitching through which to thread the elastic. *Diagram 12.* Thread soft elastic through the casing and draw up to fit the waistline. Cut off the surplus elastic and stitch the ends together firmly.

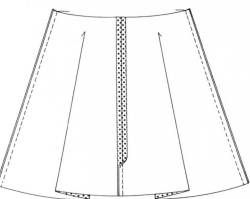

11 joining skirt pieces

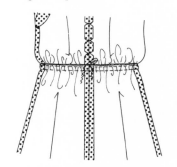

12 making the waistline casing

Finish the hem of the dress according to the instructions given on pages 43 to 46.

Luxury Travel Coat

The pattern is very simple with a raglan sleeve. But since mohair is an expensive fabric, it is a good idea to try out the pattern first using an old sheet, for example. This way, you can check the length as well as the general fit and make any necessary adjustments before you cut into the mohair.

Make up this coat pattern in a brushed mohair and it really is luxury! It is an unlined coat with an attached scarf collar and the use of a mohair fabric makes it a lightweight coat to snuggle into as well as being very warm. (Photograph page 28.)

MATERIAL REQUIRED
3.20 metres fabric 140cm wide (with or without nap)
5 × 2cm buttons
1.20 metres softline vilene interfacing

MAKING THE PATTERN
Using dressmaker's squared paper, ready ruled into 5cm squares, copy the pattern in the diagram so that the outline in each square corresponds exactly. Mark the position of the notches and the buttonholes. Cut out the pattern.

CUTTING OUT
Following the cutting layout given, place the pattern fabric pieces with the pile on the fabric running downwards, as indicated by the arrow. Cut the scarf piece twice with the un-notched edge to the fold as shown. Place the centre back of the coat to the fold. 1.5cm turnings are allowed throughout.

Cut the facing piece also in softline interfacing. Cut two strips of softline interfacing 5cm deep and 7cm wide for the top of the pockets.

pattern layout
sizes 12 and 14 ——————— *solid line*
sizes 16 and 18 – – – – – – – *broken line*
1 square = 5cm

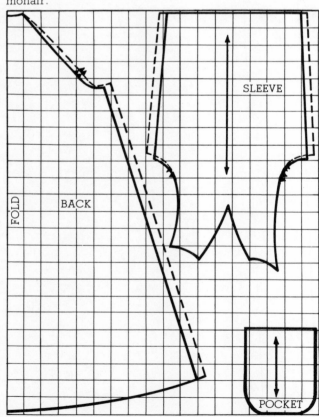

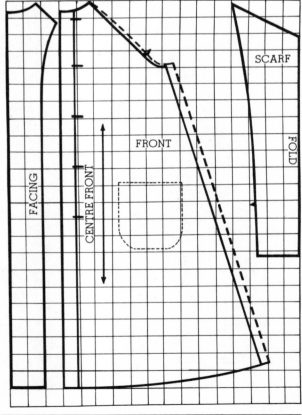

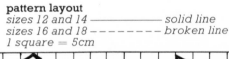

SEWING INSTRUCTIONS

The pockets Neaten the top edge of the pocket with a single turning and edge stitch. Catch stitch the interfacing to the top of the pocket 1cm down from the edge on the wrong side of the fabric. *Diagram 1.*

Fold the interfaced section of the pocket to the right side. Stitch at each side, taking a 1.5cm seam. *Diagram 2.*

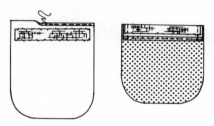

1 turning down top edge of pocket and catch stitching interfacing

2 stitching sides of interfaced section of pocket

Trim the seam to 6mm. Turn the interfaced edge to the inside of the pocket. Turn under 1.5cm round the curve of the pocket. Tack and press. *Diagram 3.*

3 tacking turnings round pocket curve

Pin the pocket on to the coat as marked. Tack and edge stitch in place by machine.

Stitch the back to the fronts at the side seams. Press open. *Diagram 4.*

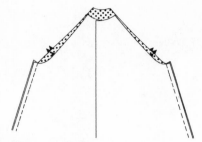

4 stitching coat back to fronts

Neatening the seams As this is an unlined coat, the inside seams should be made as neat and inconspicuous as possible. This can be done by binding the seams using a matching seam binding. *Diagram 5.* Or, by turning in 3mm at the seam edge and stitching very close to the edge. The seams are then catch-stitched invisibly to the coat fabric to keep them flat. *Diagram 6.*

The sleeves Ease the curved edges of the sleeve head together forming a dart. Stitch, taking a 1.5cm seam tapering to a very fine point. *Diagram 7.* Press the seam open.

Stitch the underarm sleeve seam and press open.

With the right sides together, pin the sleeve to the armhole edges, matching the underarm seams and the notches. Stitch, taking a 1.5cm seam and finishing the stitching on the coat front 1.5cm away from the neck edge. *Diagram 8.* Clip seams if necessary. Press and neaten.

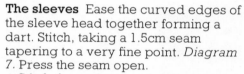

8 stitching sleeve to armhole

5 neatening inside seams with seam binding

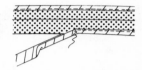

6 catch stitching inside seams to keep them flat

7 stitching sleeve darts

If making bound buttonholes, refer to the instructions given on page 66 and make the buttonholes before front facings. Machine or hand-worked buttonholes are left until the coat facing is completed.

cutting layout *140cm wide fabric (with nap)*

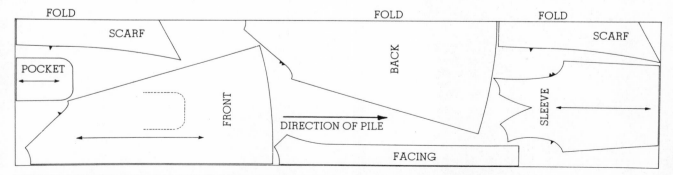

Over: left, checked and plain luxury travel coats right, nightdresses

9 *neatening edge of front
facing with seam binding*

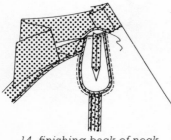

14 *finishing back of neck*

Measure the hem
following the directions
given on page 44. Open
out the front facing to
complete the hem and
then fold it back to the
inside and slip stitch in
place. *Diagram 15.*

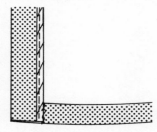

15 *slip stitching coat
facing at hem*

Refer to page 55 for
hand-worked
buttonholes. Sew on
buttons to correspond on
the centre front line of the
left front.

The coat facing Pin and tack the
softline interfacing to the wrong side
of the coat facing. Neaten the curved
edge of the facing and the shoulder
edge as before. *Diagram 9.*

With right sides together, tack the
facing to the coat front. Stitch, taking a
1.5cm seam, down the centre front
edge and along the neck curve as far
as the front sleeve seam. *Diagram 10.*
Trim the seams to 6mm and cut off the
corners.

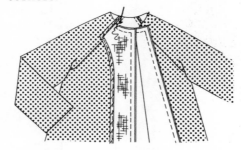

10 *stitching facing to coat front*

Turn the facing to the inside.
Diagram 11. Work the seam between
the finger and thumb so that it lies
exactly on the edge. Tack along the
edge to hold it in place. Press. Remove
the tacking and press again, if
necessary, to remove the imprint of
the tacking.

11 *turning facing to inside*

The scarf Stitch the short centre back
seam of the scarf, taking a 1.5cm seam
and press open. Fold the scarf in half
lengthwise with the right side to the
inside and stitch across each end and
along the open edge, but leave open
between the notches. Clip the seam

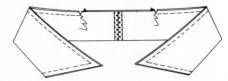

12 *stitching scarf leaving opening
between notches*

turnings to the stitching line at the
notches. *Diagram 12.* Cut off the
corners.

Turn the scarf right side out and
press.

With right sides together, pin one
open edge of the scarf to the neck
curve, matching the centre back
seams and the notches with the front
shoulder seam. Tack and stitch taking
a 1.5cm seam. *Diagram 13.*

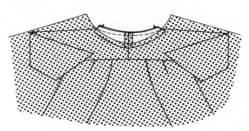

13 *stitching scarf to back of coat neck*

Press under 1.5cm on the other open
edge of the scarf. Bring this folded
edge down to the stitching line and
hem in place. *Diagram 14.*

Before turning up the hem, allow the
coat to hang on a coathanger for at
least a day. This is essential with a
mohair fabric particularly as the
hemline will drop considerably.

Mark the length of the sleeve and
trim the surplus fabric to leave a
turning of 4cm. Cut a strip of softline
interfacing 3cm deep and long enough
to go round the sleeve edge and
overlap slightly. Tack the interfacing
to the wrong side of the sleeve 4cm
away from the raw edge. Catch stitch
in place. *Diagram 16.* Neaten the raw
edge of the sleeve with a simple
turning or binding. Fold the hem to the
inside concealing the interfacing and
invisibly slip hem in place.
Diagram 17.

16 *catch stitching softline interfacing for
sleeve hem*

17 *turning up sleeve hem concealing
interfacing*

Introducing Paper Patterns

Choosing your correct pattern size, how to take your measurements

Graph patterns are a convenient and a cheap way of presenting a very simple pattern, but they have their limitations. As soon as you become more confident and enthusiastic about dressmaking, you will want to progress to a wider choice of styles and to more fashion conscious designs than it is possible to present in grid form.

This is one of the most enjoyable stages in making your own clothes – leafing through the glossy pages of the pattern catalogues with their colourful choice of up-to-date designs or more classic styles, shown in exciting fabrics and all available in a wide range of sizes.

But how do you know whether a style will suit you? How do you decide which pattern size to choose? Or, which make of pattern to choose? And to a beginner, a paper pattern with its own special language and strange pattern markings can seem very confusing.

So in the next few chapters, several STYLE patterns are discussed in detail – nothing too difficult, but good designs which should tempt the most timid home dressmaker.

But first things first – which pattern size do you choose?

CHOOSING YOUR CORRECT PATTERN SIZE

The most important thing about your pattern is not the style – it's the size! Whether or not you are in the forefront of fashion isn't going to matter at all if, after hours spent dressmaking, the finished product doesn't fit.

So it is very important to buy a pattern in the size that is nearest to your own. STYLE paper patterns come in a very wide range of sizes so that it should be possible to select a pattern which needs only a minimum of alteration, if any. It is knowing which size to choose that can be the problem.

You must first take your own measurements, very accurately. Wearing only your usual foundation garments and your slip take the following measurements and write them in pencil on the measurement chart. Hold the tape snugly, but not tightly.

Select the type and size of pattern in which measurements most closely correspond to your own.

Before you cut out your pattern compare the sleeve and finished length of the pattern with the measurements on your own personal chart.

For instructions and Your Personal Measurement Chart please turn to page 69.

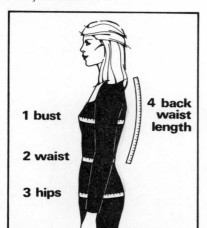

1 bust
2 waist
3 hips
4 back waist length

How to take your measurements

A Casual Jacket

Understanding paper patterns, cutting out, thread marking

STYLE PATTERN No 3140
Almost all beginners at dressmaking start by choosing to make a skirt. This isn't, in fact, the easiest garment to make without help. A skirt has to fit at the waist, have a neat zip, a straight hem and straight side seams, so that you can be in difficulties right away.

Why not try this stylish blouson jacket if you haven't much sewing experience and no one to help you? If it is successful, go on to make the easy pull-on pants that are included in the pattern and when you become more confident, you can attempt the straight skirt with a side slit. You then have an up-to-date and very useful co-ordinated outfit which, incidentally, would cost considerably more to buy than it does to make.

The jacket has four main pattern pieces and a pocket piece. It is easy fitting with a raglan sleeve which is the simplest type of sleeve there is. It has an open ended zip, which is easier to handle then a closed zip and a neat two-piece hood which replaces a collar and is much easier to attach.

The jacket is lined. This sounds more ambitious than it really is as the lining is made up in exactly the same way as the jacket and it conceals all the seams and raw edges to give a very neat professional look to the finished garment.

So, how much fabric, what kind of fabric and what else will you need?

This is where your pattern will help you.

UNDERSTANDING YOUR PATTERN
There is a good deal of helpful information on the back of the pattern envelope itself before you even open it. Have a look at it. *Diagram 1.* From this you will be able to discover
1 The number of pieces in the pattern. A beginner should avoid a pattern with too many pieces.
2 The number of garments you can make from your pattern. These are shown by line drawings as well as a brief description of each garment.
3 The kind of fabric to choose.
4 The other items you will need to buy to complete the garment – zips, elastic, thread, etc.
5 The amount of fabric you will need. To find this, circle the view of the garment you are making and the width of your fabric. Follow a line across from your fabric width and down from your pattern size. Circle the amount given where these two lines meet.
6 The amount of interfacing (if any) you will need to complete the garment is given.
7 The finished length of your garment, or in the case of trousers, the side leg length and width of each leg. It is helpful to compare this with your own garment length, as it may affect the

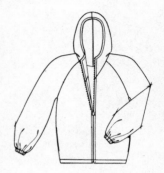

1

3140
10 PIECES

MISSES' JACKET, SKIRT AND TROUSERS: Lined jacket with raglan sleeves elasticated at wrists, side seam pockets and front zipper fastening has hood and yoke cut all-in-one. Both views are worn with purchased shoulder pads. View 1 hood is lined with fleecy fabric. Skirt has hemline split and zipper fastening in left side seam. The trousers have elasticated waist.

Suggested fabrics — Flannel, tweed, gabardine, corduroy, double jersey. VIEW 1 HOOD LINED WITH CONTRAST FLEECE.

To complete garment — Thread. View 1 and 2: 65 cm open-end zipper. 2.5 cm wide elastic, shoulder pads (raglan sleeve type). Skirt: 20 cm zipper. Trousers: 2.5 cm wide elastic to fit waist.

POCKET   WAISTBAND

FRONT   BACK   SLEEVE   HOOD   FRONT   BACK   FRONT   BACK

No allowance made for matching plaids, checks, stripes or large patterned fabrics.
For fabric with nap, pile, shading or one-way design: use nap requirements and nap layouts.

STANDARD BODY MEASUREMENTS					
Bust	83(32½")	87(34")	92(36")	97(38")	cm
Waist	64(25")	67(26½")	71(28")	76(30")	,,
Hip	88(34½")	92(36")	97(38")	102(40")	,,
Back — neck to waist	40.5(16")	41.5(16¼")	42(16½")	42.5(16¾")	,,
Fabric required	**Size**	**10**	**12**	**14**	**16**
View 1 and 2 Jacket Even check or plain fabric					
90cm(35"36") with or without nap	3.00	3.00	3.00	3.40	m
140cm(54") with nap	1.90	2.00	2.00	2.10	,,
140cm(54") without nap	1.90	1.90	2.00	2.00	,,
View 1 Lining					
90cm(35"36") without nap	2.30	2.30	2.30	2.70	,,
140cm(54")	1.30	1.40	1.40	1.40	,,
Hood lining					
140cm(54") with or without nap	0.60	0.60	0.60	0.70	,,
View 2 Lining					
90cm(35"36") without nap	2.90	2.90	2.90	3.20	,,
140cm(54")	1.80	1.80	1.90	1.90	,,
Skirt					
90cm(35"36") with or without nap	1.60	1.60	1.60	1.60	,,
140cm(54") with nap	0.90	0.90	0.90	1.00	,,
140cm(54") without nap	0.80	0.80	0.80	1.00	,,
Interfacing Woven or non-woven					
82,90cm(32"35"36")	0.20	0.20	0.20	0.90	,,
Trousers					
90cm(35"36") with or without nap	2.40	2.50	2.50	2.50	,,
140cm(54") with nap	1.60	2.00	2.10	2.10	,,
140cm(54") without nap	1.30	1.30	1.60	1.80	,,
Finished back length: View 1 and 2	68	69	70	70	cm
Skirt	66	66	66	69	,,
Side length of trousers from					
waistline marking	106	107	107	108	,,
Width at lower edge: Skirt from 98 to 112 cm; Each leg of trousers from 37 to 39 cm.					

Opposite: plain and checked casual suits

amount of fabric you need to buy. This is written below the fabric chart on the envelope back.

Inside the pattern envelope

Opening up a crisp new pattern is exciting for an experienced dressmaker, but it can be daunting for a beginner.

Take it slowly. Take time to familiarise yourself with your pattern. It is packed with all the information you need to help you cut without a qualm and put together the garment pieces easily and correctly. Rather like a jigsaw, the pattern went together well when it left the design studios. It will do the same for you if you take time to understand the instructions.

First, open out the instruction sheets (the primer). In the top left-hand corner of one of these sheets you will find a list of the pattern pieces that you will need for the garment you are making. Below this are the pattern shapes and these are identified by a letter. *Diagram 2*. Select the tissue pattern pieces for the garment you are making, ticking them off against the list as you do so. Put the others back into the pattern envelope.

The cutting layout

The cutting layout is the next thing you need to find. Look for
1 The garment you are making
2 Your pattern size
3 The width of the fabric
Find the cutting diagram which relates to these and mark it clearly. *Diagram 3*.

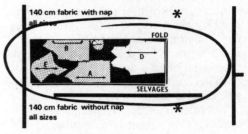

3 cutting diagram

The pattern markings

Now take time to study the information at the top of the cutting layout page. For example, it makes things very much simpler when you realise that, with your STYLE pattern, a shaded pattern piece is a piece which has been reversed, i.e. placed printed side down.

This is done to make more economical use of the fabric.

There are also several markings on your pattern, with which you should familiarise yourself before beginning to place the pattern on the fabric.

1 **The straight grain** – this arrow indicates the straight grain of the fabric. The pattern piece must be placed on the fabric with this arrow parallel to the selvage (the finished edge of the fabric). *Diagram 4*.

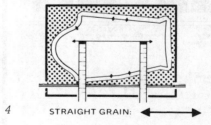

4   STRAIGHT GRAIN:

2

Select **PATTERN PIECES** for the garment you are making.

10 pieces given
view 1–2 _____ A B C D E
skirt _____ F G H
trousers _____ K L

jacket · skirt and trousers

A · FRONT   B · BACK   C · POCKET   D · SLEEVE   E · HOOD

H · WAISTBAND

F · FRONT   G · BACK   K · FRONT   L · BACK

2 The fold – the edge of a patterned piece marked in this way must be placed exactly on the fold of the fabric. This fold in the fabric is not cut. *Diagram 5.*

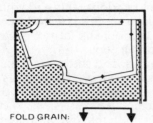

5   FOLD GRAIN:

3 The cutting line – this is indicated by a solid line and a small pair of scissors. *Diagram 6.*

6

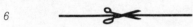

4 The stitching line – this is indicated by a broken line and a small machine presser foot. *Diagram 7.*

7

5 Pattern lengthening or shortening lines – these are indicated by a double line. *Diagram 8*

8

6 The notches – these are very important balance marks shown as projections on the cutting lines. Each notch has a number and it is matched up to the same number on another pattern piece. *Diagram 9.*

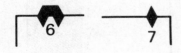

9

These are markings you need to know *before* you can cut out your pattern. The other pattern markings, known as construction symbols, are needed after you have cut out – at the thread marking stage.

YOUR FABRIC
After you have studied your pattern, have a look at your fabric. Smooth it out on a flat surface. Has it
1 A pattern that runs only one way, e.g. an uneven check or flowers 'growing' in one direction? *Diagram 10.*

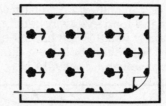

10

2 A shiny finish, e.g. satin or brushed denim or a furry pile, known as nap, e.g. velvet, mohair or corduroy?

If your fabric comes into neither category, then it presents no problem. If it does, then it is obvious that the garment must be made up, and therefore the pattern placed on the fabric, with the nap or one-way design running in the same direction on all the pattern pieces. Cutting layouts which show all the pieces pointing in the same direction are labelled 'with nap'.

The cutting layout for the jacket of STYLE pattern no 3140 gives an example of a layout using a nap fabric and a fabric without nap. *Diagrams 11 and 12.*

140 cm fabric with nap
all sizes

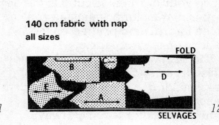

11

140 cm fabric without nap
all sizes

12

CUTTING OUT
With some knowledge of the pattern markings and any problems your fabric may present, cutting out is now relatively simple. The golden rules are:
1 Always keep the fabric absolutely smooth and flat, pinning the edges together with pins approximately 10–15cm apart. Straighten the ends of the fabric if necessary.
2 Follow the cutting layout, beginning with the grain arrows on the pattern, placing them as explained previously.
3 Having positioned the arrows, pin out the rest of the pattern, with a pin in each corner and plenty of pins on the curves. Place the pins inside the cutting line and at right angles to it.
4 Cut through the pattern and fabric

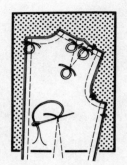

14 making tailor's tacks for construction symbols

15 cutting tailor's tacks

It is a good idea to use a different colour of thread for each of these markings and to write down on your pattern envelope the colour you have used for each.

exactly on the cutting line, using sharp scissors and long even strokes. Do not lift the fabric with the left hand. Keep this hand flat on the table near the scissors as you cut. *Diagram 13*.

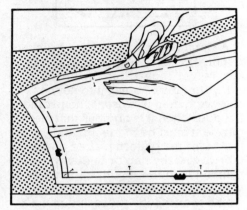

13 cutting out

5 Cut the notches outwards. If the fabric frays readily cut the notches longer than the pattern.

THREAD MARKING
Once your garment is cut out, the next step is to transfer as much as you can of the information printed on the pattern on to your fabric.

The best way to do this is by tailor's tacks. It really does simplify dressmaking to tailor tack as much and as accurately as you possibly can. Time spent tailor tacking always makes the later stages in dressmaking very much easier.

On any pattern you need to mark
1 The darts
2 The construction symbols. These are small and medium dots •   ●
3 The buttonholes (if any)
4 The centre front line on a jacket or blouse
5 The stitching line

The first three on this list must be marked with a full tailor's tack which does not fall out of the fabric readily. The last two, the stitching line and centre front line, can be marked with a quicker type of tacking, as there is so much marking involved. This quick tailor's tacking is not as secure, but it is adequate for the stitching line where it is not important if one or two tacks get lost. The centre front line should be reinforced with a single line of

tacking in a coloured thread once the pattern is removed.

Tailor's tacks for construction symbols, darts and buttonholes
1 Use a long double thread without a knot, take a small stitch through the pattern symbol and fabric, leaving an end of about 3cm.
2 Take a second stitch on top of the first, leaving a loop. *Diagram 14.*
3 Cut the thread leaving an end of about 3cm.
4 Cut through the loop and gently ease the pattern off the fabric.
5 Ease the two layers of fabric apart and snip the threads joining the layers in half, leaving a tuft of thread on both fabric pieces. *Diagram 15.*

Quick tailor's tacks for stitching lines on long seams
1 Use a long double thread without a knot. Take a small stitch on the seam line.
2 Move on approximately 5–8cm and take another stitch without cutting the thread. Continue tacking down the stitching line in this way.
3 Cut the long tacking stitches in two, and gently ease the pattern off the fabric. *Diagram 16.*

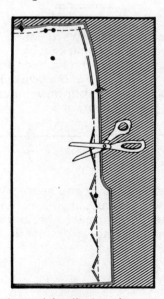

16 cutting quick tailor's tacks

4 Ease the two layers of fabric apart and snip the threads joining the layers in half, leaving a tuft of thread on both fabric pieces.

A Set of Skirts

Making your pattern fit you, concealed zips, the waistband

STYLE PATTERN No 2594
Most women would like, at least, to be
able to make themselves a skirt, and
this is a good pattern to choose for a
first attempt. It contains four different
skirt styles:
1 A four panel flared skirt
(photograph page 52)
2 A flared skirt with a centre front
pleat and side pockets
3 A straight skirt with waist shaping
darts and a centre front pleat
(photograph page 52)
4 A straight skirt which can be made
up from a metre of fabric 140cm wide
  Once you have mastered this basic
pattern, you will be able to make up
quite a wardrobe of skirts in a variety
of fabrics, from cotton to pure wool
jersey, all from the one pattern.

MAKING YOUR PATTERN FIT YOU
Buy your pattern by your waist
measurement, and then check against
the pattern measurements
1 Your hip measurement
2 Your length (the finished length of
the skirt is given on the back of the
pattern envelope i.e. with the hem
allowance turned up)

Increasing the pattern at the waist If
you are 'between sizes', e.g. if your
waist measurement is 74cm and you
are using a size 14 pattern which has a
71cm waist, you will need to increase
the pattern at the waist.
1 Divide the amount you need to add
on by four. (Since you are working on
a quarter of the pattern.)
2 Pin extra tissue paper to the pattern
margin, if necessary, at the waist.
Measure out the required amount from
the waist stitching line at the side
seams of the front and back skirt
pattern.
3 Draw in the new cutting line from
this point curving in very gradually to
the original line at the hip.
4 Shade in this area so that you do not
accidentally follow the old line when
cutting out. *Diagram 1.*

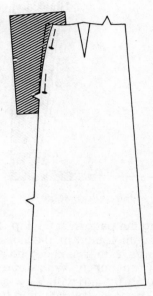

1 increasing the pattern at the waist

Adding to the pattern at the hip This
alteration is made at the side seams.
Divide the extra amount needed by
four. (Since you are working on a
quarter of the pattern.) This amount is
added to the front and the back side
seams.
1 Pin a strip of paper to the side of the
front skirt pattern. At the hipline,
measure out quarter of the
measurement needed to enlarge, from
the cutting line.
2 From this point draw a curved line
upwards tapering to nothing at the
waistline seam line. Draw a line
downwards, parallel to the edge of the
skirt, to the hem. This line becomes
the new cutting line. *Diagram 2*
(page 38).
3 Shade in the area added to the side
seam so that you do not accidentally
follow the old cutting line. Mark the
notches on the new cutting line.
4 Make the same addition to the skirt
back side seam.

Since this pattern is likely
to become one of the
most used in your
collection, it is a good
idea to cut the pattern
shapes in a lightweight
interfacing, tracing all the
markings and stitching
lines on the interfacing.
This will stand up to
constant pinning and
folding better than the
pattern tissue.

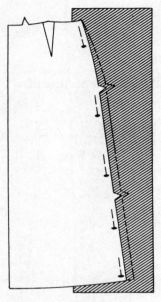

2 adding to the pattern at the hip

Reducing the pattern at the hip This is best left until you try on the skirt at the fitting stage, rather than cut the paper pattern prematurely. With some draping fabrics and with View one of this skirt pattern, you may find the skirt falls over the hips and no reduction is needed. If, however, you do need to take in the skirt at the side seams, then reduce your pattern by this amount, so that it is ready for use next time.

Lengthening or shortening the skirt Make this alteration before you cut out as it affects the amount of fabric you use.
1 To shorten – measure the amount you need to shorten the skirt from the curved lower edge of the pattern. Cut along this line.
2 To lengthen – pin paper to the lower edge of the skirt. Draw a new curved line parallel to the edge as the new cutting line. Do not rely on your memory and a chalked line on your fabric. It is all too easy to lengthen the skirt back and to forget the skirt front! And in any case, once you have made the necessary alterations to your pattern, it is ready for use next time.

CONCEALED ZIPS
All four skirts in this pattern have a zip set into the centre back seam. This means that the zip can be inserted before the side seams are joined. It

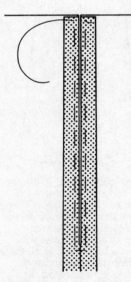

3 tacking the seam allowance

will not interfere with fitting the skirt since any further alteration will be made at the side seams and the zip is much easier to insert when you are working on a perfectly flat piece of fabric.

Putting in the zip
There are several methods of putting in a zip and this makes it all very confusing for a beginner.

It is also discouraging if a first attempt at a zip is not very successful. The finished zip should lie flat and look neat, without gaping to reveal the teeth.

What the home dressmaker really needs is a method of putting in a zip which she can master easily and which works first time and looks good.

Here is such a method. It gives a very neat concealed zip, i.e. the zip teeth and tab are completely hidden under the lap of the seam. It is suitable for every type of zip except the decorative type which is used for a front opening dress or the blouson jacket page 58, where the zip teeth lie directly underneath the line of the seam.

This method has several extra tacking stages. Don't be tempted to take short cuts and omit these stages. They will take you a little longer but if you follow these directions *exactly* you will achieve a very neat zip – at your first attempt.
1 Turn back the correct seam allowance allowed on your pattern to the wrong side. Tack along the folded edge on both sides. *Diagram 3*. Press.
2 Place the fabric on a flat table, right side uppermost.

Position the zip tab uppermost, 2cm down from the neck or waistline edge – this takes into account the 1.5cm seam allowance. Place the zip teeth as close as you can to the folded edge, without actually touching it, on the right-hand side of the garment. Pin and tack the zip in place down this edge. *Diagram 4*.
3 Exchange the presser foot on your machine for a zipper foot. A zipper foot has only one prong so that the machine needle can stitch very close to the teeth of the zip. These attachments are standard accessories on most new machines, but if you have

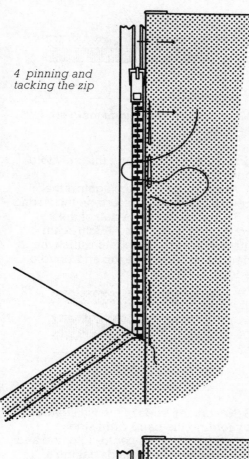

4 pinning and tacking the zip

an older machine a zipper foot can be bought separately to fit most types. It is an essential part of putting in a zip neatly by machine.

Starting at the base of the zip, stitch down the folded edge, as close to it as you can. *Diagram 5.*

4 Bring the other edge of the zip opening over to conceal the zip, with the folded edge lying exactly on top of the line of machine stitching, so that in fact you are overlapping the folded edges just a little. Tack this edge in place firmly, using short diagonal tacking stitches. *Diagram 6.*

Don't work with the garment on your knee – keep the fabric and zip as flat as possible and keep the zip closed throughout.

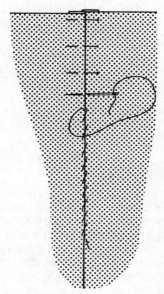

6 tacking folded edges together over zip teeth

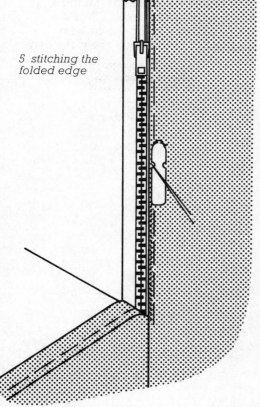

5 stitching the folded edge

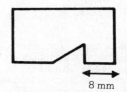

7 seam measurement guide

5 All that remains to be done now is the final stitching of the zip. This is where it is important to stitch a straight line in the correct position at the first attempt (to avoid unpicking or breaking the needle on the zip teeth!). So give yourself a guide-line to follow. For this you will need a thread that contrasts with your fabric and a seam measurement guide. These can be bought from fabric shops selling sewing aids or cut from stiff card. *Diagram 7.* Using the guide, work a straight row of tacking stitches 8mm away from the folded edge and parallel to it. *Diagram 8.*

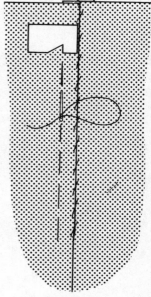

8 tacking along the guide-line

6. Using a zipper foot, machine stitch on this guide-line of contrasting thread. Stitch across the base of the zip at an angle. *Diagram 9.* Remove all the tacking threads and press the zip.

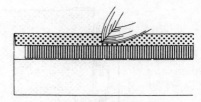

10 *pressing the seam turnings over petersham*

down the turning along this new fold line.
4 Place the petersham against the centre fold line as before on the wrong side, but on the other half of the waistband leaving the 1.5cm seam turning at each end. Catch stitch the petersham along the top and bottom edges. *Diagram 11.*

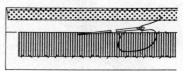

11 *catch stitching petersham*

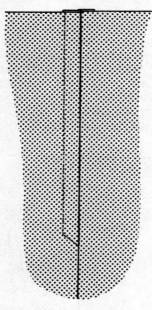

9 *stitching the zip*

A catch stitch is a diagonal tacking stitch, taking only a thread or two of the fabric into a stitch.

Pre-packed, iron-on waistband stiffenings are also available and instructions for using one of these are included in the wrap skirt pattern on page 9.

THE WAISTBAND

Some kind of stiffening must be used inside the waistband to prevent it from rolling over and to give it a crisp appearance. Petersham is one of the best stiffenings to use – several weights are available.

The waistband in this pattern has a finished width of 4cm, and it is wide enough to be worn with a narrow belt over the waistband. The band needs to be firm if it is not to crease or roll over. For a band of this type, 4cm wide petersham is the ideal stiffening.

Preparing the waistband

1 Cut the petersham to the length of the waistband, less 3cm (the seam turnings).
2 Fold the fabric waistband in half along the length, right side to the outside and press in the fold heavily.
3 Place one edge of the petersham to the fold line on the wrong side of the fabric. Pin it in place. Using the straight edge of the petersham as a guide to give an accurate line, press the 1.5cm turnings over the petersham along the length of the band. *Diagram 10.* Remove the petersham and tack

5 Neaten the ends of the waistband, by folding the band right sides together along the centre fold line and stitching across the ends, taking a 1.5cm seam. *Diagram 12.* Trim the seam to 6mm. Cut off the corners. Turn the band right side out. Press the ends.

12 *stitching ends of waistband*

Attaching the waistband to the skirt Now that you have prepared the band, attaching it to the skirt is relatively easy. Open the skirt zip and

1 With right sides together place the interfaced side of the band against the skirt waist and pin the ends of the band. For a side zip, place the end of the band exactly to the edge of the seam line on the skirt front. Allow the waistband to extend for the overlap on the skirt back. Pin, tack and machine stitch the waistband around the skirt waist, just below the petersham which acts as a stitching guide. *Diagram 13.*

13 machine stitching waistband to skirt

2 Trim the seam to 6mm. Bring the tacked folded edge of the band down on to the stitching line enclosing the seam turnings. Tack and hem in place. *Diagram 14.*

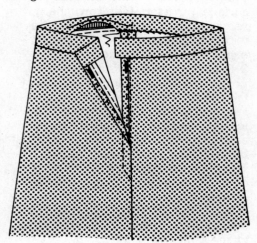

14 hemming inside waistband

3 Slip stitch the seam in the overlap together. *Diagram 15.*

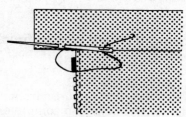

15 slip stitching overlap

4 Attach hooks and bars to fasten the band at the overlap. These will stay fastened better if they are arranged alternately, i.e. an eye to a bar and a bar to an eye. *Diagram 16.*

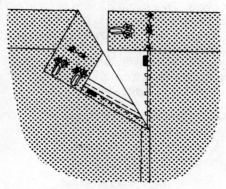

16 attaching hooks and bars

Instructions for measuring and finishing the hem are given on pages 43 to 46.

Sleeveless Cardigan and Pinafore

Choosing a check fabric, finishing the hem, top stitching

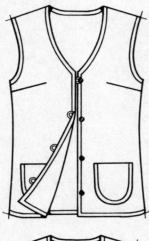

The photograph (on page 61) shows the pattern used to advantage with a check fabric co-ordinated with a plain fabric.

STYLE PATTERN No 3130
This is another STYLE pattern from which you can make up a complete co-ordinated outfit and it includes one of the most useful designs – a pinafore dress.

In the full length version, the pinafore dress has a front zip, a neat centre front pleat, a fashionable extended shoulder line and patch pockets. This same pattern is used, in a shortened version, to make the sleeveless cardigan with a button and loop fastening for wearing with a straight skirt of similar design to the pinafore with a front pleat. A trouser pattern is also included.

CHOOSING A CHECK FABRIC
There are two kinds of checks:
1 An even check *Diagram 1a*
2 An uneven check *Diagram 1b*

1a
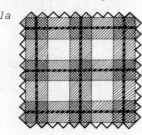

1b
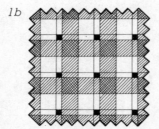

An even check Isolate a block of the check. If you start at the centre of the block, the squares or lines of the check will match, i.e. they will be the same in each direction. This is an easy type of check for a beginner to choose.

An uneven check The uneven check does not repeat its design constantly. In this case, a pattern layout 'with nap', must be followed so that the pattern pieces are placed on the fabric all pointing in the same direction (see page 35).

To complicate things further, a check can be uneven both lengthwise and crosswise. In this case, the pattern is cut singly. This kind of check is best avoided by the beginner.

Cutting out a check fabric
A check fabric must match at the seams. The sleeves should also match the bodice at the front notch. The collar should match the bodice at the centre back neck.

Since all these pattern pieces join together by means of numbered notches on the pattern, it is quite a simple matter to place those notches which correspond to each other on the same check and therefore the checks will match.

Follow these directions at the cutting out stage and you can match up the checks with confidence.
1 Smooth out the fabric on a flat surface, pin it together down the selvages and at intervals across the width, so that the check underneath exactly matches the one above.
2 Examine the fabric and plan the position of the most dominant lines of the check, e.g. the dominant lengthwise line of the check usually looks best in the centre of the garment, and the most dominant line across, just below the shoulder rather than on it. The hemline should be turned up on a dominant line to give a complete block of the check.
3 Pin on the pattern pieces, placing the corresponding numbered notches on the same line of the check. *Diagram 2.*

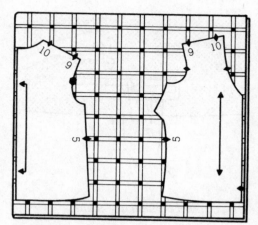

2 *pinning on pattern pieces*

If there is a bust dart in a pattern front set into the side seam, the checks will not match above the dart. This is not important since the checks will match evenly at the hem line.

4 Where there is a centre front seam (as with this pattern) or a centre back seam, take care that the stitching line falls on the centre of a block. This means that when the front or back seams are joined, they complete a block and do not disrupt the design. *Diagram 3.*

3 *positioning centre front seam*

Stitching a check fabric
Use a smaller tacking stitch than usual when tacking a check fabric and make a small backstitch at the dominant line of each check.

This will prevent the checks moving out of alignment when you machine stitch.

You may find it easier to slip tack the seams together from the right side to get an exact match.

1 Lay the two pieces side by side right side up.

2 Turn under the seam allowance on one piece and press.
3 Lay the folded edge to the stitching line of the other seam. Pin in place.
4 Take a stitch through the fold. Take a very small stitch from the under piece exactly on the stitching line and immediately below where the thread comes out of the fold. *Diagram 4.*

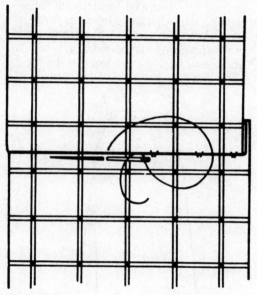

4 *slip tacking on the right side*

FINISHING THE HEM
A great deal of work can go into a hem so that no one will notice it! A good hem should be inconspicuous; it should not show as a ridge on the right side of the garment; no stitches should be visible and, of course, it should be level.

First you must decide on the length you want the finished skirt to be. To some extent, this is dictated by current fashion, but not altogether. The length to choose is the length which looks right for the garment and which gives it a good line.

Decide on the hemline length by trying on the pinafore with the shoes you will wear with it, and pin it up roughly at the front, standing in front of a long mirror. Try out several lengths by adjusting the pins, but don't bother about getting the hemline even at this stage. When you finally decide on your finished length, leave in one pin to mark this position and remove the others.

The ideal way of making sure that your finished hem is even is to stand on a firm table, and to ask a friend to mark a line round the skirt with pins, using a dressmaker's hem marker, while you stand still. A hem marker with a firm base is the best type to achieve a really even hem, but a metre stick can also be used. *Diagram 5.*

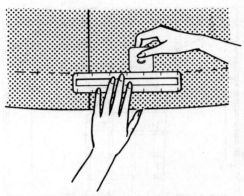

6 marking and pinning hemline

Turn up the hem on the chalk line and tack along the folded edge. Press the fold line lightly, pin up the surplus fabric on the hem and try on the dress to check the length. If no alteration needs to be made, trim away the surplus fabric in the hem evenly to 4—5cm in depth. *Diagram 7.*

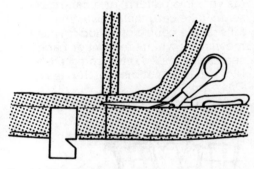

7 trimming surplus from hem

The next stage of finishing any hem varies according to the fabric and the amount of fullness in the skirt. If the skirt is straight as with the pinafore, omit stages 2 and 3.

For an A-line or flared skirt in a wool fabric
1 Trim the seam allowance inside the hem to reduce the bulk as shown. *Diagram 8.*

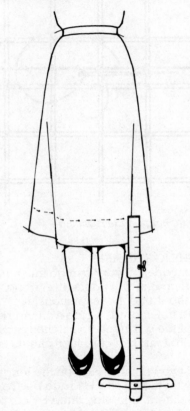

5 using a dressmaker's hem marker

Remove the pinafore and spread out the skirt on the table, and use tailor's chalk and a short ruler to join up the pins in an even curve, discarding any which are obviously out of line. *Diagram 6.*

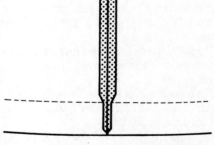

8 trimming seam allowance inside hem

2 Deal with extra fullness in the width in the hem at the seams (caused by the flared shape of the skirt panels) by running a gathering thread 7–8cm each side of the seam at the hem edge. Draw up the extra fabric with the gathering thread keeping the seam lines together. *Diagram 9.*

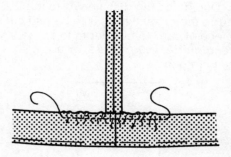

9 drawing up fullness with a gathering thread

3 Slip a piece of brown paper between the hem and the garment. Steam the gathered area using a damp cloth held over the point of a hot iron holding the iron just above, but not touching, the wool fabric. When the wool becomes damp, gently nudge the fibres together with the point of iron so that the material lies flat. With a pure wool the fullness shrinks away very easily. With a mixture of wool and other fibres more persistence is needed.

4 Neaten the raw edge of the hem with bias binding, rather than a zig-zag stitch. This will prevent the hem fullness from stretching again and it looks neater on a thick fabric. Apply the matching bias binding to the right side of the hem edge. Stitch along the crease line. Turn the binding over to conceal the raw edge and hem stitch in place on the wrong side on the line of machine stitching. *Diagram 10.*

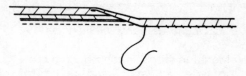

10 hem stitching binding

5 Tack the hem in place 6mm from the hem edge. *Diagram 11.*

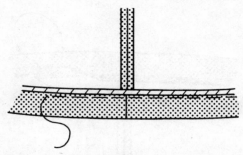

11 tacking bound hem in place

6 Turn back the fabric of the skirt exposing the hem. Using a fine needle, catch stitch the hem taking a small stitch in the underside of the hem edge, then a single thread only from the garment and so on. Do not pull the thread tight. *Diagram 12.* Remove the tacking.

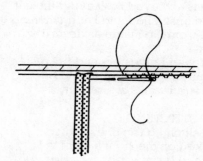

12 catch stitching

For a full skirt in a cotton or cotton mixture fabric

1 It is not possible to shrink away fullness in any fabric other than wool. Any extra fullness in the hem of a cotton skirt must be minimised by reducing the depth of the hem to 2.5–3cm.

2 Neaten the raw edge of the hem with a zig-zag machine stitch.

3 5mm away from the edge, work a single row of a straight machine stitch.

4 Tack the hem in place 6mm from the finished edge. Catch stitch the hem

The final stitching of the hem is worked from the inside. This is known as the Couture Method of stitching a hem. Using this method it is very much easier to get a neat hem without a visible ridge on the right side of the skirt.

from the inside on the line of machine stitching following the instructions for the Couture Hem. *Diagram 13.*

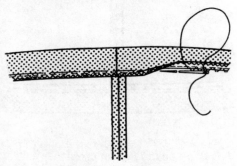

13 catch stitching

For a polyester jersey fabric Many polyester fabrics do not fray at all and it is not necessary to neaten the raw edge of the hem. A zig-zag stitch worked on a polyester jersey would stretch the hem badly. The neatest and most inconspicuous hem from the right side is achieved by leaving the cut edge unstitched and hand-stitching the hem from the inside as described above.

Woven polyesters and polyester mixtures which fray should be neatened with a zig-zag stitch.

TOP STITCHING
Top stitching is a line of stitching worked on the right side of the finished garment. Its purpose is to outline the edges, as with a collar, or to emphasise the seam line.

It is an important part of dressmaking. A straight line of machine stitching, accurately placed, on a plain fabric, will give a crisp, tailored effect. *Diagram 14.*

For really even stitching, particularly on bulky fabric, use an 'even feed' foot. This is not a standard attachment with many sewing machines, but it can be bought separately. It is helpful also for top stitching pile fabrics as the foot does not flatten or mark the pile.

14

Top stitching must be done well. The lines of stitching must be absolutely straight and parallel to the edge or to the seam line they emphasise.

To achieve perfect top stitching
1 Press the edge to be top stitched.
2 Decide on the distance from the edge the top stitching is to be and cut a piece of card to this depth to act as a seamguide, *Diagram 15,* or use a sewing gauge.

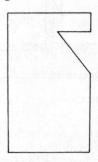

15 seamguide cut from card

On shirt blouses, dresses or safari type jackets, 6mm is a good measurement. On thicker fabrics and coats, a depth of 1cm is more effective.
3 Using a contrasting colour of thread and the seamguide, work a row of small tacking stitches in the exact position for the top stitching. *Diagram 16.*

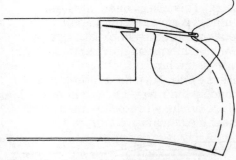

16 tacking to mark top stitching line

4 Machine stitch, stitching from the right side and using a slightly longer stitch than usual, following the contrast thread as a guide.

A Quilted Jacket and Waistcoat

Quilting, setting in sleeves

STYLE PATTERN No 3131
This is a fun pattern – as well as being a very useful one. It is ideal for the home dressmaker because there is no complex shaping by interfacing and fitting as the fabric is given support by quilting and the jacket is a simple basic shape. A long version is also included in the pattern to make a cosy, quilted coat. The edges of all the garments are finished with pre-folded braid. (Photograph page 49.)

QUILTING
Quilting is the art of stitching a light padding to a fabric to form a raised effect or a pattern.

Polyester wadding, which is washable and very light in weight, is ideal for quilting this jacket. It is sold in several thicknesses, but a 6mm depth is a good choice as it gives the effect and the necessary warmth without excessive bulk.

The wadding is usually sandwiched between two layers of fabric, and the three layers quilted together.

In this pattern, any problem with wadding in the seam turnings has been avoided by quilting only the top layer of fabric leaving the jacket lining plain. For extra warmth, you can quilt the top fabric and a brushed cotton together before the jacket is lined. If you find it easier to stitch the quilting between two layers of fabric but do not want the extra warmth, use a fine nylon net or voile as a backing.

When quilting any garment it is a good idea to cut out the pieces slightly larger than the paper pattern. Then, when the quilting is completed, replace the pattern on the fabric and cut the pieces accurately to size. Wadding is sold up to 150cm wide, so that it is possible to pin the fabric to the wadding and cut the two out together.

PREPARING THE FABRIC
The stitching lines for the quilting in this pattern are placed 7cm apart. Tack the wadding to the wrong side of the fabric round the outside edges. One diagonal line of tacking across the fabric in each direction will help to hold the wadding firmly.

1 Slacken the tension on the machine a little.
2 Reduce the pressure of the presser foot.
3 Keep to your usual size of stitch length.
4 Use the quilter attachment for your machine – this has a short, open toe which does not catch in the wadding – setting the spacing guide to 7cm.
5 Stitch with the padded side uppermost, guiding the work with both hands placed on the fabric to ensure even quilting. *Diagram 1*.

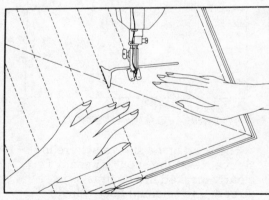

1 quilting

The collar
The collar on this jacket needs no additional interfacing as the quilting gives the fabric sufficient support. So it is a particularly easy collar for a beginner to attempt.

SET-IN SLEEVES
The sleeves are set into the jacket in the usual way, although they are cut with slightly less fullness over the

Clever effects can be achieved by a combination of plain and print fabrics or cotton and waterproofed nylon used together and the garment can be made fully reversible. In this case, the wadding must be cut out of the underneath seam turning and the raw edge of the other seam turned under and hemmed over the top. This gives a very neat seam.

Use matching thread or contrasting thread for quilting and test a line of stitching on a scrap of fabric before you quilt the garment pieces.

If you do not have a quilter attachment, it is probably better to tack down the stitching lines first. This not only ensures that they will be really even, but helps to flatten the wadding if you are stitching with the usual presser foot on the machine.

sleeve head, because of the support given to the fabric by the quilting. The sleeves of the lining are also stitched before the lining and jacket are put together. The same basic rules apply when setting in any sleeve, but if you have not set in a sleeve before, tackle the quilted sleeve first. The extra support in the fabric makes it easy to handle.

Setting in the sleeve

Setting the sleeve into the armhole of the dress or jacket seems to be the bogey for many home dressmakers and the dressmaking process which they least enjoy.

But it isn't difficult. After all, when the pattern left the makers, the sleeves fitted into the armholes exactly. And if you are accurate at the cutting out stage and transfer all the markings from your pattern on to your fabric, then your sleeves will fit also.

Your sleeve, cut out and after thread marking (see page 36) should look like this. *Diagram 2.*

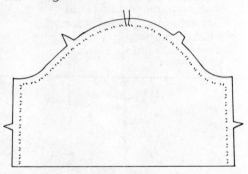

2 sleeve showing thread markings

The head of the sleeve, where the sleeve meets the shoulder seam, is clearly marked in a contrasting thread. The stitching line with the seam allowance of 1.5cm is marked by thread. Notches are also cut out in the fabric; a single notch denotes the sleeve front, a double notch denotes the sleeve back.

All these points should also be marked to correspond on the armhole edge of the garment. *Diagram 3.*

The next stage is to join the underarm seam of the sleeve and press it open.

If you now place the sleeve flat on a table, fold it in half and smooth the sleeve away from the underarm seam

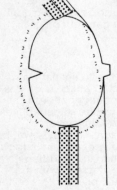

3 armhole showing thread markings

you will see that one underarm curve is deeper and more hollowed out than the other. The deeper curve is the front of the sleeve and, of course, also has the single notch. *Diagram 4.*

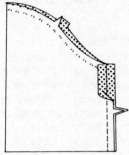

4 checking sleeve

When both sleeves are at this stage, and if you are using a fabric which looks the same on both sides, it is a very good idea to lay the sleeves flat in this way and check that in fact you have a right sleeve and a left sleeve. *Diagram 5.* It is all too easy to stitch the underarm sleeve seam to give two identical sleeves.

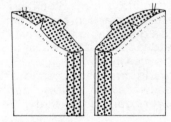

5 right and left sleeves

Before starting to insert your sleeve, run a gathering thread, by hand, round the head of the sleeve, so that it draws up readily. Start at one of the notches, and with a large knot in the end of the thread make a row of very small running stitches along the seam allowance line as far as the other notch. Leave the end of the thread loose to draw up the fullness. *Diagram 6.*

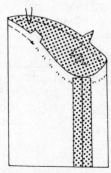

6 gathering thread round the head of the sleeve

Opposite: quilted waistcoat and coat

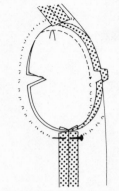

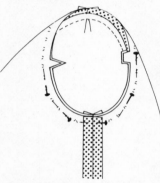

7 *securing underarm seams with a pin*

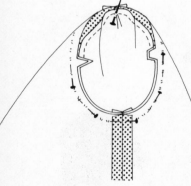

8 *pinning underarm seams*

9 *pinning head of sleeve to shoulder line*

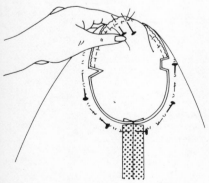

10 *easing away fullness in the sleeve head*

Once you have prepared the sleeve put the sleeve right side out on the correct arm, i.e. put your left sleeve on your left arm. Then put the arm still wearing the sleeve, through the corresponding armhole of the garment, with the garment right side out also. Take off the sleeve and the garment together holding the two underarm seams firmly together. Secure these two seams at once with a pin. *Diagram 7.*

Your sleeve and garment are now in the best position for you to begin putting in the sleeve. Both the sleeve and the garment are right side out, but you will now be looking into the wrong side of them both.

1 Pin the sleeve and the garment together round the underarm curve. Make sure that the seam lines are matching. Start at the underarm seam and pin as far as the single notch. Then go back to the underarm seam and pin as far as the double notch. *Diagram 8.*
2 Pin the mark at the head of the sleeve to the shoulder line. *Diagram 9.* When you are working with fullness like this, put the pins in at right angles to the seam line.
3 Ease the gathering thread a little. Take care not to pull up the sleeve too much – it should not be made smaller than the armhole.
4 The knack of putting in the sleeve successfully lies in the way you adjust the fullness over the sleeve head. Start from the pin at the top of the sleeve head. Work down one side of the sleeve, still looking into the sleeve head, and matching the seam allowance lines and bending the fabric of the sleeve head together with the garment over the forefinger. Put in a pin at right angles. Work down from this pin using the same procedure, bending the two layers of fabric over the forefinger. Put in a pin. This is easing away the extra fullness in the sleeve head. *Diagram 10.* Work down one side of the sleeve to meet the pins at the underarm. Go back to the top of the sleeve and work down the other side in the same way. The fullness of the sleeve head is then evenly adjusted. *Diagram 11.*

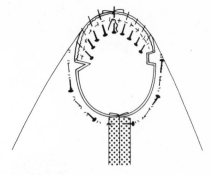

11 *adjusting fullness in the sleeve head evenly*

5 Tack round the sleeve, using a small tacking stitch, on the seam allowance line. Remove the pins and thread markings.
6 Try on the garment. Check that the sleeve is hanging correctly and that the fullness over the sleeve head is smooth and even. Machine stitch on the seam allowance line stitching from the inside of the sleeve, with the sleeve head uppermost, so that you can check that the presser foot of the machine is not pushing the slight extra fullness of the sleeve head into small pleats.
7 Remove all the tackings and press the underarm of the sleeve only. The armhole seams are not pressed open. Pressing rarely improves the sleeve head and heavy pressing can spoil the smooth rounded effect you have tried so hard to achieve. The sleeve turnings will lie naturally towards the the sleeve. The turnings should be neatened together with a zig-zag or overcasting stitch.

The jacket edges
The jacket edges are neatened with pre-folded braid. This must be carefully tacked before stitching with the slightly wider edge to the inside of the garment. If your machine has a zig-zag, it is a help to use a zig-zag stitch for stitching round the edges of the braid. Otherwise, careful stitching from the right side exactly on the edge of the braid is necessary to avoid the stitching missing the edge of the braid in places.

A Set of Blouses

Interfacing, cuff openings, hand-worked buttonholes

STYLE PATTERN No 2986
These are flattering blouses in a very feminine style. They are designed specifically for soft fabrics, such as viscose, crepe or jersey and although only two blouses are shown in the photograph on page 53, four styles can be made up from this one pattern.

Two clever design features are incorporated in the pattern. The front yoke is formed by a dart at the neckline and is cut in one with the front bodice; and the clever rever collar is simplified by a facing cut in one with the blouse front. The pattern also includes a roll collar version and a short and long sleeve.

WHAT IS INTERFACING?
Interfacing is a special fabric used in small areas of a garment to give it shape and to prevent it stretching so that it keeps that shape, as with the collar. It is also used to give a crisp edge and extra firmness where it is needed, as with the front button opening of the blouse, particularly on a soft fabric.

Which fabrics are used for interfacing? If you pick up an old sewing manual you will find that it suggests many different interfacing fabrics, buckram, organdie, net and so on. Today things are simpler for the home dressmaker. There is a special non-woven interfacing fabric made from a blend of various fibres and sold under various trade names, e.g. Vilene. It is made in several weights and thicknesses to cover all types of fabric.

The range of interfacings available includes a very sheer interfacing especially for use on fine fabrics, and several lightweight and medium weight interfacings for similar weights of fabric and a very firm interfacing for heavy fabric. There is also a stretch interfacing available which gives excellent results with jersey fabrics.

Which weight of interfacing do you choose? Choose the interfacing that is just lighter in weight than the weight of your fabric. The interfacing should support the fabric but not dominate it. If you are uncertain, drape the fabric over the interfacing in the shop, to see if it gives the effect you want before you buy it.

Sew in or iron-on interfacing? Several of these interfacings are available as iron-on interfacings, which make them quicker to apply. The choice is entirely a personal one as they both do the job equally well. But it is not advisable to use iron-on interfacings on very large areas or on garments which will be washed frequently by machine. However, iron-on interfacings used according to the manufacturers' instructions (a hot, dry iron, a damp cloth and even pressure with an up and down movement, not an ironing movement) give very satisfactory results.

Making the collar using sew-in interfacing
Cut out the collar in interfacing using the paper pattern as a guide. Tack this to the wrong side of one collar section. Machine stitch along the seam line between the small dots to secure the interfacing at the neck edge. *Diagram 1.* Clip the seam line to the small dots. Cut away the interfacing between the clips along the neck edge, very close to the stitching line.

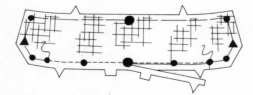

1 securing interfacing at neck edge

Fitting problems are minimised with this gathered style of blouse, so it is a wiser choice for a first attempt at a blouse than the more fitted shirt blouse. But it is important, whichever type of blouse you make, to achieve a neat tailored collar which will maintain its crispness even after repeated washing. For this reason, interfacing is used in the rever and the roll collar.

Iron-on interfacing is useful in other areas of dressmaking, e.g. strengthening the fabric for making a buttonhole and in any detail where it is necessary to clip the seam line, as with the neckline of this particular blouse pattern.

*Over: left, straight and four-panel skirts
right, rever and roll collar blouses*

2 Press under 1.5cm between the small dots. Trim the turning to 6mm and tack in place over the interfacing. With right sides facing, pin and tack the collar sections together. Stitch round the outer edge between the triangles.

3 Trim away the interfacing in the seam turning as close as possible to the stitching line. Trim the seam turnings to 6mm. Layer the seam by trimming one seam allowance slightly less to about 3mm. *Diagram 2*. Cut off the corners close to the stitching line.

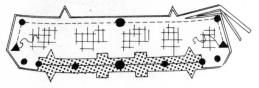

2 layering the collar seam

4 Turn the collar right side out. Work the seam between the finger and thumb so that it lies exactly on the edge. Tack along the edge to hold it in place. Tack the raw edges together and press the collar.

THE CUFF

The opening for the cuff in this sleeve is a very simple faced opening.

It is very important to clip the fabric very close indeed to the point of the line of stitching so that the fabric does not pucker when the facing is turned to the wrong side. It will help to press a lightweight iron-on inter-facing over the area to be slashed.

1 Cut a strip of lightweight iron-on interfacing 11cm long and 1cm wide. Using a damp cloth and a hot iron, press the strip centred over the slash line marked for the opening, on the wrong side of the fabric. *Diagram 3*.

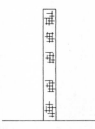

3 interfacing on the slash line

The type of opening used for a shirt cuff is given on pages 59 to 60.

2 Tack the sleeve facing over the marked opening to the right side of the fabric. Stitch each side of the slash line, tapering to a point.

3 Slash the opening on the line marked and very close to the stitching at the point. *Diagram 4*.

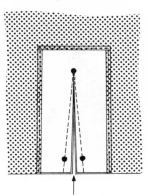

4 slashing the opening

4 Turn the facing to the inside of the sleeve, work the stitching line between the finger and thumb so that the seam lies exactly on the edge. Tack in place and press the opening completely flat. *Diagram 5*.

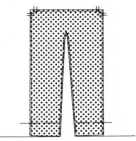

5 tacking the opening right side out

Full instructions for setting in a sleeve are on page 48 and for attaching the cuff on page 60.

BUTTONHOLES

On the soft fabrics used for this blouse, the buttonholes can be made by hand or by machine. Bound buttonholes are not suitable. Buttonholes are not one of the easiest dressmaking techniques. To make a really neat buttonhole you will need to practice on a sample piece of fabric before you try the buttonhole on the blouse. Probably more than any other dressmaking procedure a buttonhole needs practice.

So, start your practice buttonhole when you have plenty of time and when you can concentrate on mastering a new technique.

Hand-worked buttonholes

These are worked once the garment is finished and used on fine fabrics such as cotton, fine wool, silk and polyester.

1 First measure and mark the exact position of the buttonhole according to your pattern using a line of coloured thread.

2 Reinforce the wrong side of the buttonhole area by inserting a small strip of Wundaweb fusible fleece between the facing and the blouse front to cover the cutting line. Press, using a damp cloth, so that the fabric of the blouse and the facing are fused together at the buttonhole. This reinforces the area and makes the buttonhole easier to handle and to stitch.

3 Machine stitch each side of the cutting line for the buttonhole and 3mm away from it, using a small machine stitch. *Diagram 6.*

6 machining round cutting line of buttonhole

4 Cut the buttonhole along the cutting line.

5 Work the buttonhole from left to right and begin at the inner left-hand edge, i.e. nearest the side seam. Insert the needle into the back of the work and bring out the thread at the inner cut edge. Insert the needle just below the line of machine stitching and bring the double end of the thread round and under the point of the needle. *Diagram 7.* Pull the thread through forming a knot. The stitch should be upright and the knot should be eased to lie exactly on the cut edge of the work. Work along the

7 inserting needle

buttonhole edge in this way, making sure the stitches are upright and the thickness of the thread apart.

6 At the right hand edge of the buttonhole (nearest the centre front) do not make a knot on the cut edge. There is not enough room for the knots to lie neatly on the fabric. Work several simple oversewing stitches around the corner of the buttonhole. *Diagram 8.*

8 buttonhole and end stitches

7 Turn the work so that you continue to work from left to right along the other side of the buttonhole, wrapping the double end of the thread around the point of the needle forming a knot as before.

8 When both sides are completed, work a bar at the inner edge of the buttonhole. Take four stitches across the end to form four threads together lying flat against the work. Insert the eye of the needle under these threads with the single thread underneath the eye as the needle is pulled through, forming a blanket stitch. *Diagram 9.*

9 working bar at end of buttonhole

Work along the bar easing the stitches very close together.

9 Take the thread through to the back of the work and work along the four strands of thread to form a bar on the back of the buttonhole also. Press the buttonhole.

Use a matching mercerised cotton thread (polyester threads are springy and tend to knot). Use enough thread to complete the buttonhole without a join.

Jumpsuit

Welt pockets, front zips, shirt sleeve openings, attaching cuffs

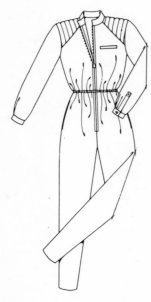

STYLE PATTERN no 2993
This is a very comfortable and easy garment to wear, especially made in glazed cotton or velour. It can also be made up in more exotic fabrics or in a polyester jersey for informal evening wear.

A WELT POCKET

If you are using a glazed cotton or a firm fabric for the jumpsuit, it is not necessary to interface the welt of the pocket. But in a soft fabric and all types of jersey fabric, a lightweight interfacing added to the welt will keep it from stretching in wear.
1 Cut the interfacing to the fold line of the welt and catch stitch it in place invisibly along the fold line. *Diagram 1*.

This pattern incorporates much of the teaching learnt from previous garments in the book. It is not a pattern for a beginner, but nor is it a difficult pattern. The jumpsuit features a quilted yoke, which is stitched in exactly the same way as the quilted jacket on page 47; it has set-in sleeves, a mandarin-type collar and an elasticated waistline – all of which have been included in previous chapters. The welt pocket and shirt-type cuff and front opening zip are new and they are attractive design features of this pattern.

It is a good idea to lightly pencil the exact position of the stitching lines given on the pattern on the interfacing, so that you get accurate stitching and neat corners.

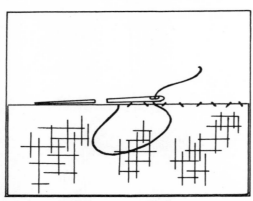

1 catch stitching interfacing to fold line of welt

2 Fold the welt along the fold line with the right side to the inside. Stitch across the ends, taking a 6mm seam. Trim away the interfacing in the seam line, close to the stitching. *Diagram 2*.

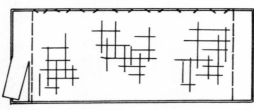

2 trimming away interfacing from seam line

Cut off the corners at the fold line only and turn the welt right side out. Press. Tack the open edges together along the seam line.
3 To reinforce the cutting line for the pocket, cut a strip of lightweight iron-on interfacing 2cm wide and 10cm long. On the wrong side of the fabric, centre the strip over the stitching lines marked for the pocket so that it extends beyond the stitching line at each end. Press it firmly to the fabric using a damp cloth and a hot, dry iron. *Diagram 3*.

3 interfacing in place on cutting line of pocket

4 On the outside of the bodice, pin the seam line of the welt along the stitching line of the pocket, matching the dots on both pattern pieces. *Diagram 4*.

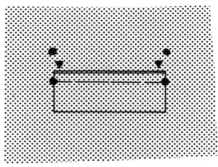

4 pinning seam line of the welt

5 Pin and tack the upper pocket over the welt matching the dots. Stitch exactly on the marked stitching line, starting in the middle of one side. Cut between the two stitching lines cutting

Opposite: plain and checked jumpsuits

into the corners 6mm from each end. Cut well into the corners as far as the stitching line. *Diagram 5.*

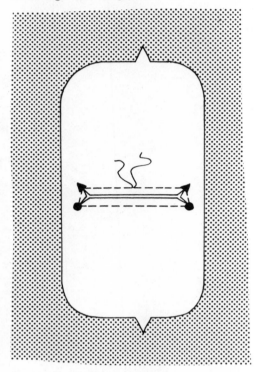

5 upper pocket in position, sewn and cut

6 Turn the upper pocket to the inside through the opening. Tack the curved edges of the pocket together and stitch round the outside of the curve taking a 1.5cm seam. *Diagram 6.*

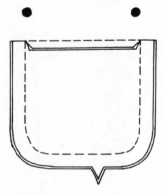

6 stitching round pocket curve

7 On the right side of the bodice, press the welt upwards. Tack in place and stitch through the thickness of the welt and fabric very close to the ends. *Diagram 7.*

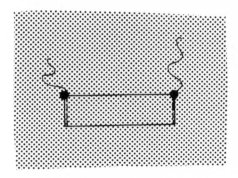

7 stitching ends of welts

A FRONT ZIP

A front opening zip is a decorative as well as a functional feature in a design, therefore, it has to be neat. The teeth of the zip are centred under the seam line and not hidden under the overlap as in the concealed zip on pages 38 to 40.

The zip should be put in closed, keeping zip and fabric as flat as possible throughout and the top stitching must be absolutely straight.

1 Tack the seam allowances of the front opening for the zip together. Tack exactly on the seam line, taking a 1.5cm turning and use a small running stitch. Press the seam open.

2 Lay the garment flat on the table, wrong side out and the centre front seam uppermost. Insert a piece of stiff card or folded thick brown paper, or a magazine between the zip opening and the underneath layer of fabric. This enables you to keep the garment flat for working and pin the zip without catching in the back of the garment.

With the wrong side of the zip uppermost position the zip tab 2cm from the neck edge. Fold the zip back on itself and gradually roll the zip down on to the seam line so that the teeth are centred exactly over the seam. Pin at intervals, inserting the pins at right angles to the zip. *Diagram 8.*

3 Still keeping the zip and garment as flat as possible, tack the zip down each side through the three thicknesses, zip tape, seam turning and fabric. *Diagram 9.*

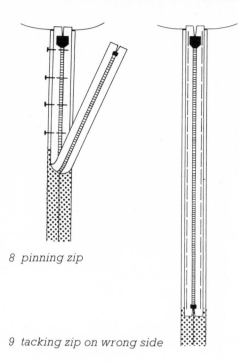

8 pinning zip

9 tacking zip on wrong side

4 Turn the garment right side out. Using a contrasting thread, make a line of tacking on each side of the seam line and 6mm away from it. Use a seam guide or tape measure to give an exact straight line, which acts as a guide for the final top stitching. *Diagram 10.*

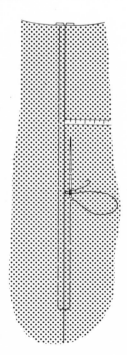

10 tacking zip on right side

5 Exchange the usual machine presser foot for the zipper foot. Machine stitch the zip following the guide line of contrasting thread. Stitch across the end just below the teeth. *Diagram 11.* Remove the tackings to open the seam and press the zip.

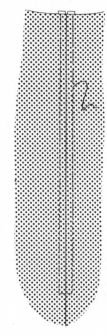

11 stitching zip

A SHIRT SLEEVE OPENING
This type of opening involves a little more work than the usual slit opening used in a blouse sleeve. It is a faced opening, similar to that in a man's shirt, with the facing turned to the right side of the sleeve, giving a very neat finish. It is easier to make any sleeve opening before stitching the underarm seam, so that the fabric can be laid flat for working.

1 Mark the length and position of the opening on the sleeve. Press a small square, about 1cm, of lightweight iron-on interfacing to cover the end of the cutting line on the wrong side of the fabric. This reinforces the weak point in the opening.
2 Slash the opening on the cutting line. *Diagram 12.*
3 Neaten the back edge of the slash with a narrow hem. *Diagram 13.*

12 slashing shirt sleeve opening

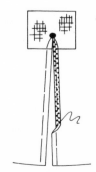

13 narrow hem on shirt sleeve opening

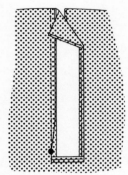

14 stitching facing strip

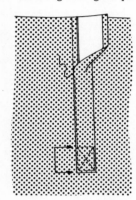

15 top stitching facing strip

4 Cut a strip of fabric 6cm wide and the length of the slash plus 3cm. Pin this strip to the front edge of the slash with the right side next to the wrong side of the sleeve. Stitch, taking a 6mm seam.

5 Turn under 6mm on the sides and top edge of the strip to neaten. Tack and press these turnings. *Diagram 14.*

6 Bring the overlap to the right side of the sleeve. Fold it in half, bringing the tacked edge over to conceal the stitching line.

    Tack in place and continue the tacking to form a rectangle projecting beyond the slit. Tack this down on to the sleeve.

7 Top stitch the tacked edges of the overlap and across the end of the slit to hold the underlap in position. *Diagram 15.*

THE CUFF

Attaching a cuff is fiddly. Very often there is quite a lot of fullness in the edge of the sleeve which has to be eased into the folded band of fabric which forms the cuff. It is therefore easier to cheat a little and stitch the sleeve on to this flat strip of fabric and then fold it back to form the cuff.

1 Fold the cuff in half along its length with the right side outside and press.

2 Cut a strip of lightweight interfacing the size of the folded cuff. Open out the cuff and place the interfacing to the fold line. Catch stitch the interfacing at the fold line. Tack it in place around the other three sides.

3 Turn under 1.5cm to the wrong side on the edge without the interfacing and tack in place. *Diagram 16.*

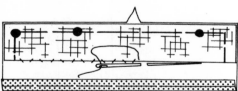

16 attaching interfacing and turning up single edge of cuff

4 Place the interfaced section of the cuff to the sleeve edge with right sides together. Tack and stitch taking a 1.5cm seam. Cut away the interfacing in the seam. Trim the seam turnings to 6mm. Press the seam towards the cuff. *Diagram 17.*

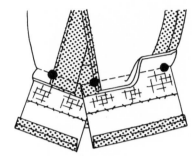

17 attaching cuff to sleeve

5 Fold the cuff back on itself with right sides together. Stitch across the ends. *Diagram 18.* Trim the seam to 6mm and cut off the corners.

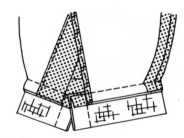

18 stitching ends of cuff

6 Turn the cuff to the right side. Bring the folded edge down on to the stitching line and hem in place. *Diagram 19.*

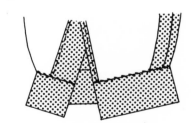

19 hemming inside of cuff

A Couture Suit

Lining skirts and jackets, shoulder pads, bound buttonholes

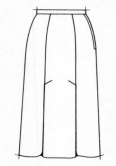

The pattern gives scope for clever combinations of colour and fabric. For example, the skirt and jacket can be made of the same fabric and a contrasting fabric used for the blouse, and this blouse fabric can also be used to line the jacket; or, the jacket can contrast with the skirt and a braid trim can be used on the jacket edges to pick up the colour of the skirt. (Photograph page 64.)

STYLE PATTERN No 3002
This is a satisfying outfit to make up. The cardigan style jacket is easy and flattering to wear and teams up with the pleated skirt and tie neck blouse to make a very useful classic outfit that will not date, but will give you years of wear.

The jacket and skirt are both fully lined. If you have not lined a garment before, then this is an excellent pattern on which to start as the jacket is lined in the simplest way. The lining is identical to the jacket, which is cut without facings, so that the lining comes to the jacket edge.

LININGS
Lining makes a garment easier to wear – it slips on and off more readily. It also looks neater, since all the seams are hidden, and the garment wears and keeps its shape longer.

You do not have to choose the traditional shiny lining fabric – although obviously a slippery fabric is easier to wear. The lining fabric deserves as much thought as the main fabric. It should be lighter in weight than the main fabric so that it will not distort it or add too much bulk.

A good choice for a lining, especially if you are using the same fabric for the blouse is a pure silk. Viscose or polyester crepe would also be a good and less expensive choice. Choose a fabric that is 'kind' to the skin and will not rustle when you move and one that does not crush readily. It should have the same washing properties as the main fabric.

Lining a skirt

All skirts are improved by the addition of a lining, with the exception of bias cut styles. A lining improves the hang of a skirt, making it more comfortable to wear. It also does away with the need to wear a slip.

For a straight or an A-line skirt The lining is cut out using the skirt pattern, omitting the waistband and shortening the pattern by the depth of the hem.

For a very flared skirt It is better to reduce the fullness in the skirt by folding in the pattern from the hip line to the hem as in the diagram. *Diagram 1.* This removes some of the fullness, giving a straighter skirt for the lining pattern, but keeps the waist and hip measurement the same.

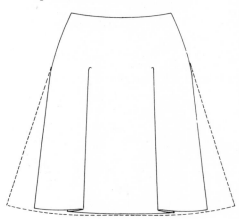

1 reducing fullness in skirt pattern for lining

For a pleated skirt Where a separate lining pattern is not given, pin in the pleats on the pattern and cut the lining identical to the skirt, omitting the pleats and shortening the lining by the depth of the skirt hem allowed on the pattern. It is a good idea to cut out the lining fabric using pinking shears, as some lining fabrics fray very readily.
1 Cut out the skirt lining from the pattern allowing 2–3mm on the side seams to give the lining a little more 'ease' than the skirt.
2 Make up the skirt as far as, and including, the zip. Make up the lining in the same way as the skirt, leaving an opening for the zip in the right side seam.

3 With the skirt wrong side out and the lining right side out, slip the lining over the skirt. Match any darts and the seams, and pin and tack the lining and skirt together at the waistline.

4 Fold back the seam allowance of the lining fabric at the zip opening. At the base of the zip, snip the lining at an angle to the seam allowance. *Diagram 2*.

2 snipping lining at base of zip

Turn under the raw edges and hem the folded edges down on to the zip tape. *Diagram 3*.

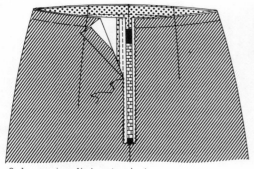

3 hemming lining to zip tape

5 Attach the skirt waistband including the waist edge of the lining with the skirt.

6 Turn up the hem of the lining so that the finished hem is 3–4cm shorter than the finished hem of the skirt. The lining hem can be finished by hand or machine.

A machine embroidery stitch, such as a scallop stitch, makes an attractive finish to the hem. Where a fine lining fabric has been used the hem can be finished with matching lace. *Diagram 4*.

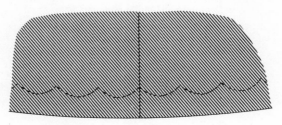

4 finishing lining hems with machine embroidery (above) and lace (below)

7 Work bar tacks, approximately 1cm long between the lining and the skirt at the side seams just above the hem, to hold the lining in place. *Diagram 5*.

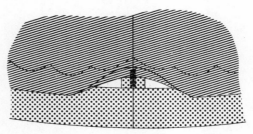

5 attaching bar tacks to skirt and lining

These are worked in the same way as the belt carriers for the jacket. *Diagram 6*.

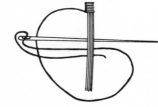

6 working bar tacks

Lining a jacket

With this simple cardigan type jacket, the lining can be made up, complete with sleeves, and put in all in one. An alternative method which gives good support to a loosely woven fabric is to insert the sleeves last, by hand, so that the jacket and lining seams can be fixed at the armhole where there is extra strain.

A pleat allowance is made at the centre back of a jacket or coat lining so that the lining is not restricting in wear.

1 Cut out the lining, placing the centre back edge of the jacket pattern to the fold of the fabric, and 2.5cm away from it. *Diagram 7*. Before removing the pattern, tack in this pleat down the length of the jacket back, parallel to the pattern edge.

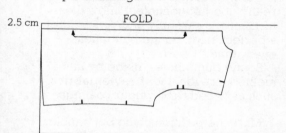

7 placing pattern on fabric for jacket lining

2 Stitch the pleat to secure it, at the neckline, waist and hem edge, with a short line of stitching in these three areas, about 2.5cm long. *Diagram 8*.

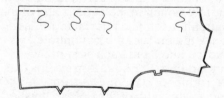

8 stitching centre back pleat

Press the pleat to one side. Once the lining is inserted the tacking thread is removed to release the pleat.

3 Make up the lining in the same way as the jacket, but do not put the sleeves into the lining. Make any alterations that were made to the jacket to the jacket lining also.

4 Pin and tack the lining and jacket with right sides together and stitch round the outside edges, leaving an opening. Turn the jacket right side out through the opening.

5 Using a matching thread and a small running stitch, stitch the lining to the jacket round the armhole edges 6mm away from the edge, matching the shoulder and underarm seams. *Diagram 9*.

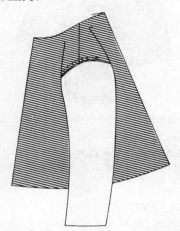

9 stitching lining to jacket round armhole edges

6 Turn under the 1.5cm seam allowance on the sleeve round the sleeve head and tack in place.

7 Place the front sleeve seam of the lining to the front sleeve seam of the jacket with wrong sides facing. Check that you have the correct sleeve for the arm. Stitch the seams loosely together with a diagonal tacking stitch. *Diagram 10*.

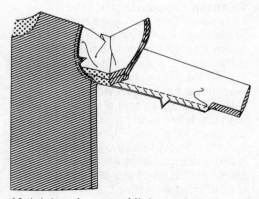

10 joining sleeve and lining seams

A dressmaker's dummy is invaluable when lining a jacket. A well padded coathanger is a substitute.

Opposite: couture suit colour combinations

8 Slip your hand down inside the sleeve lining from the armhole and turn the sleeve lining right side out, drawing it up over the jacket sleeve. Hem the sleeve in place round the armhole, easing in the fullness over the sleeve head. *Diagram 11.*

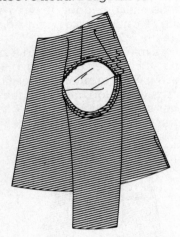

11 hemming sleeve round armhole

9 Turn under the raw edge of the lining and slip hem the lining over the sleeve hem.

SHOULDER PADS
Shoulder pads are used as a fashion accessory to give a square-shouldered look. They also firm up the shoulder and sleeve head and help the garment to keep its shape. Shaped shoulder pads made from foam are readily available. They are lightweight and washable. If they are to be used on an unlined garment, cover them with matching fabric. If a thicker pad is needed, shoulder pads can be easily made from one or more layers of wadding.

To attach a shoulder pad The thickness of the pad goes to the edge of the sleeve seam, and the circular thinner edge extends towards the neck edge to support the shoulder.
1 Fold the pad in half and mark half way along the thicker edge.
2 Place the mark to the shoulder seam with the edge of the pad to the edge of the seam turnings.
3 Stitch the edge of the pad to the seam turnings using a loose stab stitch. Stitch the curve of the pad to the shoulder seam with a back stitch. *Diagram 12.*

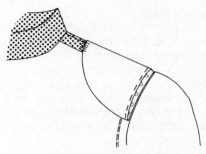

12 stitching shoulder pad to shoulder seam turnings

BOUND BUTTONHOLES
The most commonly used method of making a bound buttonhole requires very careful stitching to give a neat result. The method given here is a similar method, but it has several extra stages included. This means that it takes a little longer to complete, but it is a foolproof method of making a really good buttonhole. Follow these instructions carefully and you will get a perfect, neat, bound buttonhole every time.

Bound buttonholes, made by this method, are ideal for heavier fabrics, such as tweeds and velour coatings.

1 Mark the position of the buttonholes accurately on the right front of the garment with a line of coloured thread.
2 On the wrong side of the garment, press on a small square of iron-on interfacing (approximately 5cm square) to cover the cutting line of the buttonhole and the surrounding area. Lightly pencil in the cutting line of the buttonhole on this interfacing. Also mark the ends of the buttonhole and mark a line 5mm each side of the cutting line. For finer fabrics this can be reduced to 3mm. *Diagram 13.* This rectangle is the outline of the finished buttonhole and it is a good idea to

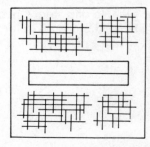

13 interfacing and buttonhole cutting lines

pencil in all the buttonholes at this stage so that you can check that they are all the same length and equidistant.

3 Cut a square of the garment lining large enough to cover the buttonhole area (approximately 5cm). If the garment is not to be lined, use an extra-lightweight interfacing. Centre the square of lining over the buttonhole on the right side of the garment and tack in place.

4 Using a small stitch, machine stitch round the outline of the buttonhole. Start in the centre of one long side; make good right angled corners by leaving the needle in the work and swivelling the fabric at the corners; count the number of stitches taken across the short sides to ensure that both ends are uniform. *Diagram 14.*

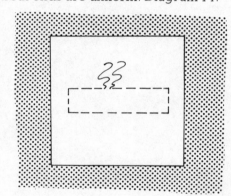

14 stitching round outline of buttonhole

5 Slash the buttonhole along the cutting line, stopping within 6mm of the corners. Cut outwards into each corner, almost to the stitches. *Diagram 15.*

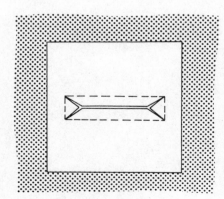

15 cutting buttonhole opening

6 Turn the lining through the opening to the wrong side of the garment. Pin it so that it holds back the turnings, forming a good rectangle, and no lining shows on the right side. Press the opening.

7 Cut two squares of the garment fabric 4cm wider and longer than the buttonhole. Place them right sides together. Tack along the centre using a small stitch. *Diagram 16.* Press the tacked seam open. *Diagram 17.*

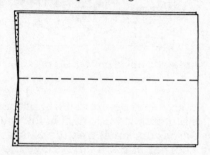

16 tacking fabric patch for buttonhole

8 Centre this patch of fabric behind the buttonhole opening so that the tacked line is exactly parallel to the sides of the rectangle, forming the lips of the buttonhole. Pin in place. *Diagram 18.*

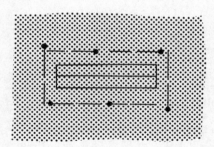

18 pinning fabric patch behind buttonhole opening

9 With wrong side of the buttonhole facing you, turn back the fabric to reveal the seam turnings. Remove the pin from one long side and using a back stitch or a stab stitch, stitch by hand immediately above the machine-stitched line, through all layers, iron-on interfacing, fabric, lining and fabric

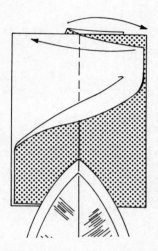

17 pressing fabric patch

patch. Stitch well into the corners.
Diagram 19. Make sure that you stitch
only just above the machine-stitched
line, i.e. away from the cut edge. This
ensures that no lining is seen on the
right side.

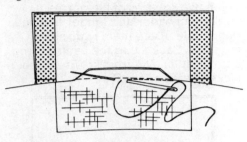

*19 hand stitching seam turning of
buttonhole*

10 Remove the pin from the short side
of the buttonhole and stitch in the same
way across the small triangle of fabric
at the corner immediately above the
machine-stitched line, through to the
fabric of the lips of the buttonhole.
Diagram 20.

20 hand stitching short side seam

11 Continue right round the
buttonhole in this way. Trim excess
fabric from the lining and patch and
press the buttonhole. Remove the
tacking which holds the lips of the
buttonhole together.

To finish the back of buttonhole
Fold the garment facing, or, in this
pattern, the jacket lining, over the
buttonhole and tack in place. Mark the
position of the buttonhole by stabbing
four pins through to the facing from
the right side of the buttonhole
marking the outline of buttonhole at
each corner. Cut a line between these
pins cutting outwards at the corners,
as in *diagram 15* of the instructions on
page 67. Turn the raw edges under
and hem in place.

Your Personal Measurement Chart

Name _____

Date _____

Height (without shoes) _____

BODY MEASUREMENTS

1 Bust
Around fullest part, straight across
back, high under the arm _____

_____

2 Waist
Comfortably, at natural waistline _____

_____

3 Hips
Around fullest part, approximately
20–25cm below waist _____

_____

4 Back waist length
From prominent bone at back neck
base to waistline _____

_____

THESE MEASUREMENTS SHOW
My figure type is _____

in pattern size _____

Other measurements – to compare
with the pattern measurement

SLEEVE LENGTH
a) Shoulder to elbow _____

b) Elbow to wrist _____
Take with arm bent – to establish
correct location of sleeve darts

FINISHED DRESS LENGTH
From nape of neck to hem _____

BACK SKIRT LENGTH
From waistline to bottom of skirt, down
centre back _____

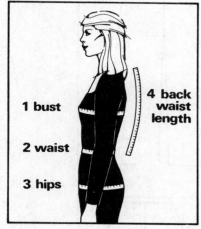

How to take your measurements

These are the measurements on which
your pattern size has been based.

At the back of the STYLE catalogue
you will find a complete range of all
the pattern types and sizes including
men's and children's sizes. But the
range from which you will select your
own pattern size is:

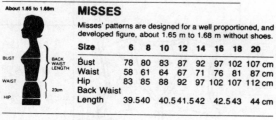

MISSES

Misses' patterns are designed for a well proportioned, and
developed figure, about 1.65 m to 1.68 m without shoes.

Size	6	8	10	12	14	16	18	20	
Bust	78	80	83	87	92	97	102	107	cm
Waist	58	61	64	67	71	76	81	87	cm
Hip	83	85	88	92	97	102	107	112	cm
Back Waist Length	39.5	40	40.5	41.5	42	42.5	43	44	cm

WOMEN

Women's patterns are designed for the larger, more fully
mature figure, about 1.65 m to 1.68 m without shoes.

Size	40	42	44	46	48	50	
Bust	112	117	122	127	132	137	cm
Waist	94	99	105	112	118	124	cm
Hip	117	122	127	132	137	142	cm
Back Waist Length	44	44.5	45	45	45.5	46	cm

Select the type and size of pattern in
which measurements most closely
correspond to your own.

Before you cut out your pattern
compare the sleeve and finished
length of the pattern with the
measurements on your own personal
chart.

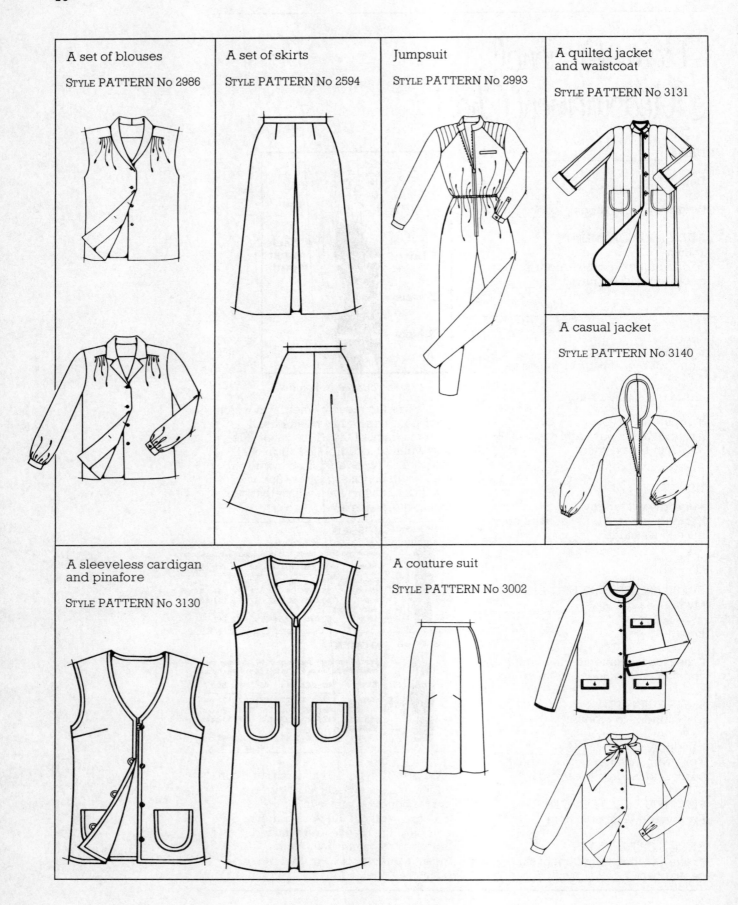

A set of blouses

STYLE PATTERN No 2986

A set of skirts

STYLE PATTERN No 2594

Jumpsuit

STYLE PATTERN No 2993

A quilted jacket
and waistcoat

STYLE PATTERN No 3131

A casual jacket

STYLE PATTERN No 3140

A sleeveless cardigan
and pinafore

STYLE PATTERN No 3130

A couture suit

STYLE PATTERN No 3002

How to order your Style Patterns

Your local stockist will be pleased to supply all STYLE Patterns featured in this book.

YOU MAY HOWEVER ORDER THESE DIRECT FROM THE FACTORY
Please fill in your coupon accurately and in block letters and post your order to:
Order Department, Style Patterns Ltd, Blantyre, Glasgow G72 0XD.

Please make Cheque/Postal Order payable to 'Style Patterns Ltd'.

PATTERN NUMBER	6	8	10	12	14	16	18	20	40	42	NO OF PATTERNS ORDERED	PRICE PER PATTERN	VALUE
2594									▓	▓		£1.25*	
2986	▓	▓						▓	▓	▓		£1.10*	
2993							▓	▓	▓	▓		£1.35*	
3002	▓	▓						▓	▓	▓		£1.65*	
3130	▓	▓	▓									£1.65*	
3131	▓	▓					▓	▓	▓	▓		£1.65*	
3140	▓	▓					▓	▓	▓	▓		£1.65*	
TOTAL NUMBER OF PATTERNS ORDERED												VALUE OF CHEQUE/ P. ORDER	£

*The prices will not be valid after the 30th September 1981

NAME_____

ADDRESS _____
_____
_____
_____

NAME_____

ADDRESS _____
_____
_____
_____

PATTERN NUMBER	6	8	10	12	14	16	18	20	40	42	NO OF PATTERNS ORDERED	PRICE PER PATTERN	VALUE
2594									▓	▓		£1.25*	
2986	▓	▓						▓	▓	▓		£1.10*	
2993							▓	▓	▓	▓		£1.35*	
3002	▓	▓						▓	▓	▓		£1.65*	
3130	▓	▓	▓									£1.65*	
3131	▓	▓					▓	▓	▓	▓		£1.65*	
3140	▓	▓					▓	▓	▓	▓		£1.65*	
TOTAL NUMBER OF PATTERNS ORDERED												VALUE OF CHEQUE/ P. ORDER	£

*The prices will not be valid after the 30th September 1981